God Bless

Ann Wigmore

and

Viktoras Kulvinskas,

Prophets of Health and Spirit,

Whose Teachings

Have Given Birth

to a

New Generation of

Healers

Sprouts

The Miracle Food

The Complete Guide

to Sprouting

Sprouts
The Miracle Food
The Complete Guide to Sprouting

by Steve Meyerowitz

Sproutman®

Let Your Kitchen Be Your Garden
The Agriculture of Tomorrow is Here Today™

Illustrations by Michael Parman

http://www.Sproutman.com

Publisher's Cataloging-in-Publication
(provided by Quality Books, Inc.)
Meyerowitz, Steve.
Sprouts the miracle food : the complete guide to sprouting / Steve Meyerowitz.
–6th ed.
p. cm.
Includes bibliographical references and index.
Library of Congress Catalog Card Number : 99-90521
ISBN: 1-878736-04-3

1. Sprouts. 2. Cookery (Sprouts) I. Title.

SB324.53.M49 1999   635
                        QBI99-900713

The *Flax Sprout Bag* is a trademark name belonging to
The Sprout House and is used with permission.

Sproutman Publications
PO Box 1100, Great Barrington, Mass. 01230
413-528-5200. Fax 413-528-5201.
http://Sproutman.com   Email: Sproutman@Sproutman.com

Distributed by
Book Publishing Company
PO Box 99, Summertown, TN 38483
888-260-8458. 931-964-3571. Fax 931-964-3518
http://bookpubco.com   e-mail: bookpubl@usit.net

Table Of

CONTENTS

INTRODUCTION

SPROUT IT!

THE TECHNIQUE

GROWING GRAINS & BEANS

AFTER THEY'VE GROWN

S E E D S

NUTRITION

EARTH & WATER

INTRODUCTION

When your teeth crush an apple, say to it in your heart: Your seeds shall live in my body, And the buds of your tomorrow shall blossom in my heart, And your fragrance shall be my breath, And together we shall rejoice through all the seasons. - Kahlil Gibran

Not all of us can be gardeners. But we all eat. Fact is, if you don't grow your own, someone has to do it for you. Not a bad concept, but in reality, we're on the losing end. A trip to the supermarket proves it. The lettuce is lifeless; the spinach is wilting and dark around the edges. You don't dare eat the fruit for fear of fumigants, fertilizers, pesticides and the like. As a nation, we're eating less and less of the healthiest foods on the planet--fresh fruit and vegetables. Where are the fruits and vegetables? For the most part, you'll find them in the canned food aisle. No wonder kids grow up never liking their vegetables! Of course, you could shop at the health food store. But organic produce sometimes cost more than you want to spend-- if you can find it at all. Unfortunately, we don't all live in southern California and we don't all have the time or means to garden.

Here's where apartment gardening comes in. Every week a new harvest of fresh baby greens matures right in your own kitchen. No tools to buy, no big investment in garden equipment, no bugs or weather to worry about and no dirt. One pound of indoor lettuce takes up just 9 inches of counter-top space and one actual minute of care per day. Just dip and set. Light is no problem--normal daylight is all you need. For such little effort, the possibilities are magnificent--30 delicious varieties of fresh, nutritious indoor greens and baby vegetables, enough to feed the whole family!

I Regained My Health With This Food

I got over a life-long struggle with allergies and asthma by revamping my diet. The first thing I did was eliminate the chemically tainted produce I was bringing home from the supermarket. How could anyone ever get well with invisible ingredients like DDT, EDB, Aldicarb and Chlordane hidden in their food? But it's more than that. It's what they don't have...nutrition. Mass market agricultural techniques rob the soil of minerals and substitute synthetic fertilizers and hormones. Zinc, for example, is no longer adequately supplied in the U.S. diet. As a consequence, the American male suffers from the world's highest incidence of prostate cancer and malfunction. Whatever vitamins these vegetables do have is diminished more and more with each day they sit wilting on grocery store shelves. If you had a choice, would you regularly eat food grown 3,000 miles from where you live?

My Apartment Garden Fed Hundreds

Since I lived in an apartment, I learned to garden indoors. Before long I was dining on crisp *Chinese cabbage, luscious crimson clover, hearty sunflower, succulent buckwheat lettuce, spicy red radish, velvety kale, sweet green pea*--I had so much, I fed all my friends and students. These young greens were so alive and scintillating with color and aroma, you could practically feel their vitamins! Make no mistake about it. That vitality is assimilated by *you*--in the form of live enzymes, vitamins, amino acids, trace minerals, RNA, DNA, oxygen and other secret elements about which only nature knows. You can't buy that nutrition in a pill!

You'll Help Our Environment, Too

If you garden indoors, you effectively reduce your dependence on distant sources for food, energy and technology. Don't think the greenhouse effect is just something that exists in newspapers. Global warming, air pollution, oil spills and acid rain all damage our health as a nation and directly threaten the quality and availability of our food. Drought, flood, heat wave, freeze, increase the price of food as does the rising price of gasoline that is needed to transport it. Our system of over industrialized, long distance, imported, chemically laden, synthetically fertilized and artificially processed foods has got to stop. Either we change it or it will change us. But what can we do about it? Fortunately, you are not completely at the mercy of the giant agri-business industry. You can take steps to become more self-sufficient. Indoor gardening is your answer and it's easier than you think.

How easy is it? The seeds do all the growing. Your only job is to water them one minute per pound per day (30 seconds in the morning, 30 seconds in evening). No weeds to weed, no pests to fence out, no bugs, no soil. It takes less time than standing on line at the supermarket! Only 5 tablespoons of seed, costing only 15-30 cents, yields a full pound of sprouted greens. Where else can you find a comparable source of fresh, nutritious food at that price? Whether you live in Metropolis on the 30th floor or in Alaska, whether it's January or July, you can have fresh food and lots of it year-round.

The World's Most Economical & Nutritious Food

Your grains, beans, and seeds can safely store for years. So next year when the price of spinach rises to $1.40 /lb., don't worry. You'll only be paying 20 cents/lb. for organically grown sunflower greens (more protein than spinach), or 25 cents/lb. for jumbo alfalfa greens (more chlorophyll and minerals than parsley). One pound of sprouts provides the combined nutritional advantage of thousands of baby plants. Biologists tell us that in the first 5-10 days, young plants achieve their maximum nutrient density. In other words, they are more nutritious than at any other point in their growth. These babies are literally overflowing with rapidly multiplying enzymes, vitamins, proteins and minerals needed for the development of the mature vegetable. B-Vitamins alone increase 300% to 1500% in just 3 to 6 days. Complex starches are broken down reducing cooking time and making beans and grains easier to digest. Enzymes abound!

You don't need a laboratory to tell how nutritious these foods are. You can taste it in their flavor, smell it in their aroma and see it in their color. When was the last time an iceberg lettuce looked delicious to you? Don't blame the poor colorless, bland iceberg. It was grown on devitalized, artificially mineralized soil worn out a hundred years ago from massive over-cropping!

All You Need To Make 1 lb of Indoor Lettuce

5 Tbsp seed (15-30¢)	Normal indoor daylight
9 inches counter space	5-10 days till maturity
1-2 minutes watering/day	A bamboo basket and greenhouse

That's all it takes to have something most people will covet--an alternative source of fresh food. In hard times, your sprouter and organic seeds can mean survival. In good times, you'll thrive in gourmet style with some of the tastiest and most nutritious foods on the planet!

What's for Dinner?

★ Cashew Cottage Cheese
★ Sour Dough Sprout Bread
★ Sprouted Wheat Breadstix
★ Dairyless Ice Cream
★ Sunflower Sun-Cheese
★ Zucchini Chips
★ Manhattan Sprout Chowder

★ Almond, Sunflower Milk
★ Sprouted Hummus Spread
★ Sunflower-Power Dressing
★ Rejuvelac-no alcohol-Wine
★ Homemade Natural Sodas
★ Beansprout Marinade
★ Banana Chip Snacks

From soups to salads, dressings to dips, sprout breads to sprout cookies, crackers, casseroles, croquettes, dairyless cheeses, naturally sweet snacks, raw juices, condiments, non-dairy homemade yoghurts, soft cheeses, ice creams and yes...even pizza. Your diet will overflow with new flavors and textures. There's a whole new cuisine of exciting tastes waiting for you and it's all derived from stored grains, beans and vegetable seeds.

Small Investment

For a small investment of $50 to $100, you could purchase all the seeds and tools necessary to cultivate hundreds of pounds of food! You can pay more than that for a lawn mower! You literally get a food factory that keeps on going and going and costs only pennies per pound. You'll grow baskets of fresh, young salad greens; eat meatless burgers made from soy sprouts, soups from sprouted lentils, sautés from sprouted green peas, snacks from sprouted peanuts, hummus from sprouted garbanzos and all kinds of sprouted breads from wheat and rye. It's so easy--just dip and hang. It's easy to establish a routine so there is always a fresh batch ready to eat. Some seeds sprout in as little as two days!

> *IT'S NOT THE FOOD IN YOUR LIFE,*
> *IT'S THE LIFE IN YOUR FOOD.*

They say that if you eat fresh, raw fruits and vegetables, you'll feel fresh and energetic. If you eat wilted, old or canned food, you'll feel...well, wilted, old or canned. Your home-grown, indoor greens are the utmost in freshness. You won't lose one precious vitamin. These baby green plants trap the energy of the sun and convert it to chlorophyll. Eating fresh, live, chlorophyll-rich foods nourishes every cell of our bodies and increases stamina.

The Agriculture of Tomorrow is Here Today

Imagine...dinner time the year 2010. You are preparing the meal of the future for you and your family. You reach out to your kitchen window and pick a handful of young lettuce greens. There is no soil; they are clean and ready to serve.

It is a beautiful vision. Every home provides its own food. Your own kitchen garden grows super-nutritious young vegetables ready to harvest in just one week. Today, kitchens serve as places to prepare food and store boxes and cans. But a 21st century kitchen generates its own food. That makes each household largely food-independent! If everyone had fresh food at home, in every season, we would have a healthier nation and dramatically lower grocery bills.

Now visualize this headline in your morning newspaper:

PRESIDENT ANNOUNCES MAJOR CHANGE
IN NATION'S FOOD SUPPLY
Use of Pesticides and Other Chemicals Discontinued
NEW CONCEPT PROVIDES FRESH FOOD
to Every Location in Every Season
Produce Prices To Drop Dramatically

Wouldn't it be miraculous if you were really reading this in your morning newspaper? This is the good news we all need to hear. Although the present likelihood of such a presidential pronouncement seems remote, you can make such a dream come true right now. The following pages tell how.

Sproutman

Steve Meyerowitz

10 Reasons To Start Sprouting!

ECONOMICS Seeds can multiply 7-15 times their weight. At $4.00/lb. for seed, that yields 26 cents for a pound of fresh sprouted indoor-grown organic greens!

NUTRITION Sprouts are baby plants in their prime. At this stage of their growth, they have a greater concentration of proteins, vitamins and minerals, enzymes, RNA, DNA, bio-flavinoids, T-cells, etc., than at any other point in the plant's life--even when compared with the mature vegetable!

ORGANIC No chemicals, fumigants or questions about certification. You can trust it's pure because you are the grower!

AVAILABILITY From Florida to Alaska; in January or July, enjoy live food anytime, anywhere, even on a boat or when hiking a mountain trail.

SPACE-TIME It's Easy! Just add water! No soil. No bugs. No green thumb required. No special lights. One pound takes grows in only 9 inches of space and takes 1 minute of care per day.

FRESHNESS Because they are picked the same day they are eaten there is no loss of nutrients sitting in crates or on grocery store shelves.

DIGESTIBILITY Because sprouts are baby plants, their delicate cell walls release live nourishment easily. Their nutrients exist in elemental form and the abundance of enzymes make them easy to digest even for those with weak digestion.

VERSATILITY More varieties of salad greens than on your supermarket shelves...including buckwheat lettuce, baby sunflower, French onion, garlic chive, Chinese cabbage, purple turnip, curly kale, daikon radish, crimson clover, golden alfalfa and more... Your salads will never be boring again!

MEALS Make sprout breads from sprouted wheat, rye, or barley. Snacks from sprouted peanuts, hummus dip from sprouted garbanzo, cooked vegetable side dish made from sprouted green peas, Chinese sautes from mung, adzuki and lentils, even sprouted wheat pizza!

ECOLOGY No airplanes or fuel/oil consumed to deliver this food to you. No petroleum based pesticides or synthetic fertilizers.

The Agriculture of Tomorrow
is here Today

SPROUT IT!

Behold, I have given you every herb bearing seed,
which is upon the face of all the earth and every tree
in which is the fruit of a tree yielding seed.
To you, it shall be for food.

Genesis, 1:29

You're in a tight spot. Inside an elevator, to be exact. The elevator is in Macy's department store in New York City. The time: the last shopping day before Christmas. Feel like a sardine? *(Apologies to vegetarians.)* Let's hope your fellow shoppers don't decide to stretch, scratch, turn, tilt, yawn or perform any other kind of bodily expansion. You'd get seriously squooshed! Now, you know what it's like to be a seedling growing up inside a jar. The world is closing in around you while your whole life's purpose is simply to seek the sun. The following pages are dedicated to the sun worshipers of the world.

Seeking the Sun

Vertical Germination Of Seeds

Sprouts are baby green plants. Like all helio-tropes, they follow the sun from dawn to dusk. Through the miracle of photosynthesis, they create their own food (carbohydrate) from sunlight. Jars are simply not designed to accommodate this natural growth process. Sprouters with a vertical orientation, on the other hand, work in harmony with the natural movement of green plants. They permit your sprout greens to grow like vegetables in your garden. In this book, we will be using a colander style vertical sprouter. Borrowing from the Orient's love of bamboo as a cooking utensil, we will use a simple, widely available bamboo basket as our sprouter in the step by step discussion of how to grow sprouted baby vegetables indoors. In this sprouter, the sprout roots support themselves by winding into the weave of the basket instead of soil. Once firmly anchored, they grow straight and stand tall. Our technique will apply to any sprouter with a vertical orientation and ample height for growth.

Multiple Generations

Multiple harvests are possible from just one batch of seeds with your colander style vertical sprouter. How is this possible? All seedlings grow straight up, but they grow at different rates. The more mature sprouts create a shield for the others. As the tallest sprouts are harvested, more light penetrates into the densely packed growing seeds enabling the next generation to rise and flourish.

A mature sprout releases its hull and opens like a flower. These little green plants represent the first generation. Like the folks in the crowded Macy's elevator, once they get off, there is more space for those left behind. Now, it is the turn of the next generation of seedlings. They are smaller and a little more yellow around the collar, but after one or two days exposure to light, they will grow as green and as tall as their elders.

A skilled indoor gardener can reap two, three or more generations from one batch of seeds, depending on the variety. This means a lot more sprouts for your dollar. For example, with just 5 tablespoons of alfalfa seed (⅓ cup), you can grow over one pound of alfalfa sprouts. Five tablespoons of seeds (about 2 ounces) costs approximately 25 cents and yields 1 pound of hearty alfalfa greens. This means your sprouts cost approximately 25 cents or less per pound. With such high yield and low cost, you could share your sprouts with friends and neighbors, eat big salads everyday for lunch and dinner, and still have plenty left over. Vertically grown sprouts are the healthiest of all. Multiple generation harvesting allows each seedling to develop its sun-derived chlorophyll and reach its nutritional peak. Look at your sprouts closely. If you examine them, you can identify this peak time according to when it throws off its hull and divides into its first pair of leaves.

Why Not A Jar

Sprouts have never been much of a political issue, but the vertical method of sprouting is truly democratic. In it, every sprout has an equal opportunity to get his or her time in the sun. Jars, unfortunately, cannot make the same offer. Instead, jars hold the sprouts captive and subject them to dark, crowded conditions. Sprouts come out twisted and confused! It is a tough life for a young sprout growing up in a jar. Only the ambitious ones make it to the jar edge where they finally get some sun. The rest live in the center where they are shielded from the sun and get little or no light at all. This is called the *tunnel effect*. When you reach in to harvest your sprouts, you cannot avoid pulling out those that are immature, yellow from lack of light and surrounded by their brown hulls. To make matters worse, consumers tend to fill their jars with too much seed. This forces the sprouts to survive in severely overcrowded conditions. It cuts down on their air ventilation, reduces drainage and can lead to overheating and rot. It also creates internal jar pressure which prevents the sprouts from developing to their full length. Sanitation problems abound because in such tight spaces, there is no room for the fallen seed jackets or hulls to go. Jar sprouts are usually short, twisted, yellow and full of hulls. They multiply an average of 7 to 8 times their volume. Vertically grown sprouts, on the other hand, are always clean, green, tall and naturally good looking. They can increase from 12 to 15 times their size.

Originally, all us sproutarians started out growing beans in a jar. But when you start getting serious about your sprouting, the limitations of the jar quickly become apparent. Jars breathe and drain only through their mouth. They must be tilted at an angle to make sure they won't collect water, but in that process the beans clog the mouth limiting the entrance of air. Jars require a lot of handling--filling, draining, tilting--and once you start sprouting lots of varieties, are very space intensive in the kitchen and refrigerator.

Vertical sprouters grow the seedlings the way vegetables grow in the garden. Each seed gets proper exposure to light and air. The seed hulls that are normally trapped inside a jar are free to fall off naturally. This makes less cleaning work for you, and the growing sprouts are free of this dead matter which can cause rot. Some of the hulls are heavy, such as sunflower shells, which become entangled in the mass of roots making the whole lot inedible. Other varieties are 4-6 inches tall and even if they could grow in a jar, would not fit. While jars are okay for basic bean sprouting, they were never intended for the more sophisticated indoor gardening of salad greens.

Advantages Of A Vertical Sprouter

1) Allows for the natural vertical growth of plants just like in a vegetable garden.
2) Provides a greater surface area exposing more sprouts to sunlight.
3) Yields a higher volume of sprouts.
4) Allows all sprouts to reach their nutritional peak.
5) Has its own drainage system, avoiding screens, cheese cloth, rubberbands, etc.
6) Allows faster, easier rinsing and cleaning of seed hulls.
7) Never needs soil.
8) Adds beauty to your kitchen and entire house.

The Technique

Create Your Own Sprouter

Gather your high germination sprouting seeds, a 16 or 32 ounce jar and obtain or devise your own vertical sprouter. You can make your own Indoor Vegetable Kit or vertical sprouter using a plastic colander or a natural bamboo basket. Make sure the openings in the basket are small enough to prevent the leakage of tiny seeds. If using bamboo, choose an unpealed fiber. The skin of the bamboo acts like a natural lacquer resisting the absorption of water. This results in better resistance to fungus growth. Choose a basket that has 2 inch sidewalls. Baskets are made from many different fibers. (See p. 26.) Make sure you have chosen bamboo.

A greenhouse can be made from anything that will hold in moisture and heat while allowing light penetration and air circulation. With some caveats, even a simple plastic bag will do. House your colander inside a plastic tent. Elevate the colander so it does not touch the floor or the walls for best air circulation. Good air circulation resists mold and fungus growth.

5 Easy Steps to Health
Green Thumb Not Required

1. Soak your seeds Overnight In A 16-32 Jar of pure water.
2. Pour Seeds Into Bottom Of Basket Sprouter.
3. Rinse Vigorously For 30 Seconds With A Sink Sprayer Moving Evenly Over The Seeds.
4. Place Basket In Greenhouse Tent With Ample Air Above Seeds.
5. Repeat 30 Second Rinsing Twice Daily, About 12 Hours Apart. Takes Only 1 Minute Per Day.

Enjoy Sensational Salads Every 6-12 Days

Wash Seeds and Baskets

First, wash all your baskets by boiling them for only 3 minutes in hot water. Boiling sterilizes the natural fibers which are untreated, unfumigated and unshellacked. More on the care and maintenance of your baskets on p. 28. Rinse your seeds clean, too. These special organically grown and chemical-free seeds may contain small amounts of soil or foreign matter. Rinse well and, if necessary, pick clean.

Soak your seeds in a 16-32 ounce jar with pure water.

Soaking Seed

Next, open a package of seeds (we recommend clover for starters) and pour 5 rounded tablespoons into a clean pint jar; fill ¾ of the jar with pure, cold water. Stir, then let sit for 6 to 8 hours or overnight.

After soaking, pour the seeds directly onto the floor of the 8 inch basket. Rinse them clean and let the spray of the water spread the seeds evenly on the floor of the basket. Insert the basket into the plastic greenhouse tent. Remove it from the greenhouse twice each day for rinsing. It's that easy! Now, the proper way to rinse.

How To Rinse

Rinse the seeds with cold water using the flexible spray hose attached to your sink. If you do not have such a hose built in, purchase a spray adaptor which easily connects to the end of your faucet. Faucet spray adaptors are available at houseware stores.

Shower your seeds and baskets with a dish hose or faucet spray adaptor. Use strong water pressure. Wash the basket walls as well as the seed. Good rinsing washes away fungi that cause mold and mildew. Wash for 10 seconds or more twice daily and no more than 12 hours between rinsings.

Shower your seeds as well as the basket walls and rims with good water pressure. Good rinsing with strong water pressure washes away the fungi that cause mold and mildew. After 2-3 days, most seeds send out roots and attempt to anchor into the basket weave. Shower the seeds evenly trying not to dislodge them in their effort to root. Leave the bed of seeds even and level. Wash for approximately 10 seconds, twice daily and no more than 12 hours apart.

Three Methods of Rinsing

1) *HOSING.* The first method, described earlier hoses the seeds with lots of water pressure from your hose sprayer or faucet spray adaptor. This is the only way to rinse during the first four days of growth until the roots anchor into the basket weave.

A shower nozzle, much like the one in your shower, performs best because it waters the seeds evenly without disturbing their orientation. Some sinks have a sprayer hose built in for doing dishes. If you do not have a shower head on your faucet, you can obtain a faucet adaptor from any hardware or houseware store. *Rubbermaid* makes a non-permanent adaptor called the *Faucet Queen* that attaches to your faucet end. Although the name may be somewhat quizzical, the function is one of converting the jet of water into a shower spray. And, with the simple turn of a valve, your faucet returns to normal again. This small $3--$5 item is available in most stores where housewares are sold. The sprouts prefer the even rinsing of a shower to the harsh drilling of a faucet. Please do not confuse a shower spray with a mister or atomizer. Misters do not supply enough force for an efficient rinse. One more point, when rinsing, you will notice that the water moves the seeds around. This is normal for the first two or three days but after that, try not to disturb the organization of the sprouts so that their roots may anchor into the basket. Anchoring is necessary for cleaning the sprouts vertical growth, and as we shall see later, for cleaning the hulls.

In case you were wondering, yes, you can use your shower itself. Sprouts like it in the bathroom because it is the most humid room in the house and is often a few degrees cooler in the hot weather. Simply run the basket under the shower and set it aside to drain. You may close the curtain if your sprouts happen to be shy. Actually, the curtain keeps in the humidity and creates a greenhouse effect.

2) *IMMERSION.* This method is faster and easier than hosing but is only possible when the sprouts have anchored their roots into the basket. This usually occurs after 4 days of growth. First, fill your sink, bowl or pot with pure water, then dip in the entire basket for a total bath. Let the sprouts soak for at least 10 seconds, then drain and set in the greenhouse. Make sure your sprouts are securely anchored into the basket before immersing. Check the underside of the basket for lots of rootlets showing through the weave.

Water temperature and water purity are important. *(See p. 134.)* The water temperature should vary according to season. In hot weather, it could be cold to cool the sprouts down. In cold weather, it could be warm to warm them up. Never use hot water which can reduce germination. Use lukewarm or tepid water.

The
Wrong
Way

*STANDARD FAUCETS ARE
INADEQUATE FOR RINSING
SPROUTS. THEY CAUSE
MOLD.*

3) *INVERSION*. Hang On Sprouts! Once your sprouts are securely anchored, you can even turn the basket upside down! Nothing will fall out except old seed hulls. Hulls are dead matter that decay promoting root rot and mold. Eliminating these hulls will keep your sprouts healthy and delicious. Fresh hulls, by the way, are simple vegetable fiber similar to bran. Although they can detract from the flavor of the sprouts, they are not harmful to eat. The inversion method is the fastest, most thorough method for rinsing away the hulls.

How to Drain

Even though they are porous, baskets will retain water if held in a level position. After rinsing your seeds, hold the basket at an angle for a minute or until it stops dripping. You can test this yourself by holding a wet basket level and then tilting it slightly. The water will start to drain as soon as you tilt. Do not tilt too much during the first few days or the seedlings will fall out with the water. They require at least three days before their roots are long enough to wrap into the weave of the basket and hold on. Placing your basket on a dish rack or leaning it on a towel is very helpful if you have a lot of baskets or simply do not want to stand and wait. Or, when the seedlings have anchored themselves, you can wave the basket gently in a tub of water with the basket turned upside down to shake loose any excess water, then insert it back into the plastic greenhouse tent.

Keep your sprouts in the kitchen, on a windowsill, or if you have a lot, in the bathtub. They grow best at a temperature of 75 degrees. Set it where there is light, although it is best to keep them out of the hot sun *(see p. 48).* Most seeds take from 5-8 days after the soaking to mature. Then you are ready to harvest.

How to Harvest

Harvesting usually brings forth images of large machinery moving through vast open fields. But to a sprout gardener, it simply means time to eat.

Time to eat. Grab your baby-greens by their tops and wiggle them free. Draw out the whole plant, roots and all. If too tight, grab a smaller amount and wiggle as you pull. Buckwheat and black skin sunflower all have long, heavy roots that can hold a strong grip on your baskets. Harvest these sprouts carefully by wiggling small amounts out at a time while holding the basket securely in place. While still gripping the sprouts, whisk the roots through a bowl of water to dislodge any hulls. Yes, you can eat the roots! These roots have never touched soil and are clean and full of minerals. This is a rare opportunity to enjoy the healthful benefits of eating a whole plant.

Some folks are not used to touching food especially if it is being served to others, however, with sprouts, it's different. What you grab ends up on your own plate, So you are not actually touching someone else's food. But if your company is fussy about fingers, pull them out for everyone and mix them in your salad bowl or set them on a salad plate where people can take their own. Unfortunately, tongs or salad grabbers do not work. Because the sprouts are rooted into the basket or colander, you need the combined strength and tenderness of the human hand. If done correctly, you will not disturb the younger, immature sprouts growing underneath. These sprouts are the next generation. Although they are light green or yellow in color, they will turn green and mature once exposed to the light. Try not to grab deep into the basket or to pull from the bottom. This makes a hole in your crop and pulls up the younger generation before it is mature. When you are finished, put your basket back in the plastic greenhouse tent and allow the immature sprouts to continue growing. If you "pluck" your sprouts properly, you can reap as many as 3 harvests depending on the variety and season. This maximization of your crop is possible simply by working with the different rates of seed growth and allowing the different generations to mature. You get greater yields and more food value from sprouts in their "nutritional prime."

When to Harvest Your Crop

Your young, leafy green sprouts are at their nutritional peak when the bud develops a cleft (divides into a left and right petal) and drops its hull. Harvest time is when 90% of the crop is hull-free and has left and right petals. Refer to the following chart. Harvest time may vary slightly depending on temperature and season.

Number of Days To Mature

5-6 Days	7 Days	8-12 Days	12-14 Days
Radish	Alfalfa	Buckwheat	Garlic
Cabbage	Clover	Fenugreek	Onion
Kale		Red Pea	Chia
Turnip		Sunflower	Psyllium
Mustard		Wheatgrass	

Harvest Times For Chlorophyll Rich Sprouts
Number of Days to Maturity.

Fenugreek	8 days	Radish	5 days
Alfalfa	7 days	Cabbage	5 days
Garlic	14 days	Onion	14 days
Red Clover	6 days	Black Mustard	5 days
Kale	7 days	Turnip	5 days
Buckwheat	10 days	Sunflower	10 days
Wheatgrass	12 days	Chia	14 days
Red Pea	11 days	Psyllium	14 days

Of course, you can eat these sprouts before they mature, but you would be losing a lot. The popularity of sprouts is based on their reputation as nutritional superfoods. But this is not the case if they are not fully mature! Their nutritional peak usually occurs at the time of their first leaf division. Many restaurants serve a salad full of brown and yellow sprouts. The brown parts are the hulls which have not fallen off yet and the yellow represents the lack of full chlorophyll development. Simply speaking, you are not getting what you are supposed to. Not only that, certain undesirable factors remain present within the seed until the plant fully develops *(see p. 113)*. Once you grow a delicious crop of mature green sprouts, you will never eat them any other way. Eating immature sprouts shortchanges you in total yield as well as nutrition. Patience pays.

What Seeds To Sprout

Your sprouter is ideal for growing indoor vegetable seeds that develop chlorophyll--rich, green leaves. These include:

Alfalfa	Garlic	China Red Pea
Clover	Onion	Turnip
Fenugreek	Mustard	Cabbage
Radish	Buckwheat	Broccoli
Kale	Sunflower	Chia

Which Seeds - Which Size - How Much

6" 2-3 Tbsp	*8" 5 Tbsp*	*9" 6-7 Tbsp*
Radish	Alfalfa	Buckwheat
Garlic	Clover	Sunflower
Onion	Fenugreek	China Red Pea
Cabbage		
Kale		
Turnip		
Chia		
Mustard		

6 INCH BASKET, 2 - 3 TABLESPOONS SEED

These varieties are hot and/or spicy. Use the smallest 6 inch basket for them unless you have a spicy appetite. Use 2-3 tablespoons of seed. Garlic, Onion, Radish, Cabbage, Turnip, Kale, Broccoli, Mustard, Canola, Chia. Garlic and onion are delicious and very hearty. Mustard is hot. Cabbage, turnip, kale, broccoli and canola are all cabbage family. Chia is a gelatinous seed *(see p. 157)*.

8 INCH BASKET, 5 TABLESPOONS SEED

Alfalfa, Clover and Fenugreek. Clover is a spicy cousin of alfalfa with bigger leaves. Fenugreek is a bitter herb and very healthy for the respiratory system. Use it mixed with alfalfa for best taste. 5 Tbsp can yield one pound of salad greens.

9 INCH BASKET, 6 - 7 TABLESPOONS SEED

Buckwheat, Black Skin Sunflower, China Red Pea. These three seeds represent the largest leaves and tallest stalks of the sprouting family. Mung beans may also be grown this way even though they are not a salad green. Choose only *whole* buckwheat and sunflower *in-the-shell*.

Double Decker Technique

Stack Your Sprouters! Since space is often a problem, here's a technique to conserve it. Two sprouting baskets on top of each other take up less space than two side by side. During the first phase of germination (days 1-4), any two of the sprouters could be stacked with the smaller basket underneath the bigger one. Insert the double decker into the greenhouse.

It's a great space saver, but that's not all. Seeds send their roots vertically downward searching for soil. The extra height of the double decker gives the roots from the top basket plenty of room to stretch. Ordinarily, they are matted underneath the basket by the floor of the greenhouse tent. Elevating the basket gives the roots space to breathe and has the potential to increase the length of the stalks.

Keep your sprouters double-deckered until the top roots start to touch the sprouts in the lower basket. With alfalfa, this occurs after about 3-4 days of growth. After that, follow the standard method of growing each basket on its own. If you wish to continue elevating the bottoms of the baskets in order to give space to the root systems, insert small sticks or stones underneath.

How To Set Up Your Kitchen

Your sprouting basket only takes up 9 inches (diameter) of space. However, if counter space is a premium or you wish to work with several sprouters simultaneously, it will be advantageous to establish a sprouting area. Usually, this can be done with a simple shelf on a window. Shelf brackets, readily available at houseware stores, make for easy installation. One or two shelves is all you will need. A hook on the shelf edge can be used to hang a sprout bag for sprouting beans. If possible, choose a window or wall that does not get direct sunshine for more than a couple of hours per day. Too much direct sun can overheat your sprouts, especially in the summertime. *(See Light p. 48.)*

The double-decker technique saves space and give more room to the roots. Good for the first few days of growth.

The Greenhouse Tent

Greenhouses can come in a variety of different sizes and shapes from the size of an outdoor structure building to a simple 10 inch plastic tent. Believe it or not, this simple plastic tent serves a very important purpose. During the first few days of their life, a sprout is highly vulnerable to the elements and its worst enemy is dry air. Seedlings are accustomed to the protection of Mother Earth. Normally the soil acts as their shield to regulate their temperature and keep them moist. But since our

The greenhouse tent with plenty of air circulation above the growing sprouts. Use the greenhouse throughout the growing stage to maintain temperature and moisture.

indoor seedlings are grown without soil, extra care is required. A greenhouse provides the necessary protection. It:

1)   Retains moisture
2)   Maintains temperature
3)   Allows light to enter
4)   Allows adequate air circulation.

Without protection, wind and air will dry your sprout garden. Both the roots and the tops are unprotected and will shrivel and dry. If you leave the greenhouse tent off for only half a day, enough damage could be done to ruin the growth potential. Even if the damage is not immediately obvious, it often becomes apparent when the sprouts do not grow as tall or endure as long. The dried sprouts go bad first and affect the health of the whole basket. This problem is especially critical during the first four days of germination when the seeds are just developing their roots and uprighting themselves. After that, the sprouts organize and send their roots down while simultaneously developing their leaf systems. Once developed, the leaves retain moisture and act as little umbrellas which shield the sprouts from wind and heat. The mature sprouts are less vulnerable and can survive even without the greenhouse tent for a few hours. The leaves can stay out in the open but the roots cannot. The roots are exposed and depend on the greenhouse to prevent them from drying out. Once you eat from the mature crop, you remove the top layer and with it a lot of pro-tective leaves. Then, they need the greenhouse once again. The greenhouse is recom-mended throughout the life of the sprouts but is less critical when the sprouts are mature and their leaf systems are fully developed.

Use the pyramid tent for the small 6 inch basket or seedlings which are very small and need little air.

A simple plastic bag can serve the role of a greenhouse as long as it is thick enough not to topple from the weight of the water droplets that col-lect inside. A thickness of 4 millimeters with a gusseted design gives it the strength and prevents collapse. An erect tent enables adequate air circulation. Insert your sprouts into the greenhouse tent in such a fashion that it stands vertically, like a tent, over the basket. This creates a large bubble of air for the sprouts to breathe and is the most critical factor in using the greenhouse. Consider the effect of a bag that sits on top of or collapses on the growing sprouts. They will suffocate and, if warm outside, quickly overheat. But if there is a sufficient envelope of air, the sprouts will breathe well and keep cool. The only time you may use a smaller tent or bubble of air is when the sprouts are just starting. One, two, and three day old sprouts can survive with less air because their respiration process is just beginning.

Make sure your baskets have drained well before putting them into the greenhouse tent. Hold them at an angle until the dripping stops (about 20 seconds). Or gently swing the basket shaking off excess water. Be careful not to shake off the sprouts! Tuck the greenhouse tent loosely underneath. It need not be airtight, but you must tuck it underneath to protect the roots. You may wish to place your basket on a few small stones to elevate it from direct contact with the plastic. Chopsticks, miniature pyramids or any suitable utensil will suffice. Please do not use a towel as protection for your furniture. The towel dries the roots. Use a surface where water is no problem. The greenhouse tents are very durable and last a long time, but should be washed periodically with soapy water and aired out to keep them clean and free of mildew. Fill your sink with warm sudsy water and immerse the greenhouse in it. Swish the bag around for a few minutes then, rinse and hang dry. For best results, turn them inside out to dry. Rinse your bags regularly and hang them out to air dry. Fungus can grow anywhere, even on plastic. Wash them whenever they smell musty or appear dirty.

☞ ☞ ☞ *USE THE GREENHOUSE TENT THROUGHOUT THE GROWING PERIOD.* ☜ ☜ ☜

Another critical factor in using a greenhouse is overheating. Heat builds up rapidly inside and the sprouts can cook and spoil. This can happen at any stage of development even from day one. Be especially careful in the hot weather. Keep your sprouts in the shade or give them light only in the late afternoon when temperatures are cooler or in the evening when using artificial Vita-lites.

Homemade Greenhouse

Want to build a more elaborate greenhouse? Simply construct a rectangular frame approximately 2 feet long by 1.5 feet wide and 1.5 feet high. Staple a plastic sheet on all sides

Homemade greenhouses can be made from a variety of materials.

except the front flap which should be hinged for taking the sprouters in and out. Now, simply set your sprout baskets inside. In cold climates, place your greenhouse tent, rigid plastic greenhouse or homemade greenhouse, near an incandescent light where the heat of the bulb will be trapped inside for faster germination. Use only an incandescent bulb. Fluorescent lights and the new compact fluorescents are highly energy efficient which is great except we need bulbs that produce heat. Neodymium bulbs are best for plants and people because they offer a fuller spectrum of light than regular incandescent bulbs. Duro-test and Chromolux are two popular brand names available through your light store. Ask them to special order it for you.

The Marriage Of Baskets & Sprouts

Baskets can mean many things to you and me. They may be something that holds your bread or something that holds your laundry. But to a sprout, a basket is a very personal thing. It is his/her home, cradle, bedroom and dining room all in one. Some baskets have weaves that are too wide. A little sprout could fall through to a frightening death! Some are woven too thick leaving no room to breathe. Some are lacquered poisoning sprouts and people. Some are too shallow. A little sprout must have it just right.

The ideal basket for a sprout is made from bamboo, a plant itself that grows in the rain forests of Asia. The vast majority of bamboo products are imported from China. Other fibrous woods such as wicker, straw, willow and rattan are not suitable. Bamboo baskets come in different sizes and shapes, but for sprouting purposes, we use one 8 or 9 inches in diameter with sides 2 ½ inches high. The weave is a tea strainer weave and the fiber is not shellacked. Larger more open weaves are necessary for big sprouts like sunflower, China red pea, buckwheat and wheatgrass that have large root systems.

A bamboo vertical sprouter is much more aesthetic than a plastic one. The sprouter itself is a plant product! The sprouts themselves are as pretty as little flowers. They stand straight and tall and in full bloom. There are no plastics, jars, metal colanders, trays or tubes to detract from their beauty. They are simple to use, take up little space and add to the decor of any kitchen or windowsill. For a natural product, baskets are amazingly long lasting. You can expect your basket to survive a couple of years and hundreds of pounds of salad. The fibers themselves remain unaffected by all the water since their natural habitat is the rain forest. Their ultimate failing is that they start to unravel with age. But then again, so do we all.

In the summertime or in hot climates, keep an end of the greenhouse tent open to enhance air circulation and dissipate the buildup of hot air.

The Darkening Basket Syndrome

In recent years, a near epidemic of chronic fatigue syndrome has surfaced in this country, making it the modern malaise of the 90's. Much can be done about it and live foods can help. Sadly, sprouts are also suffering from a chronic syndrome --the mysterious darkening "disease" overtaking their bamboo sprouter-homes. Many have fretted over this problematic plague, but hold on to your hulls, we've rounded up the suspects.

The culprits? Black oil sunflower, striped sunflower, black buckwheat, garlic chives and french onion. Here's how we caught 'em. We tested each of these seeds in new baby clean bamboo sprouters and watched them leach their natural pigments into the bamboo.

These seeds are among the largest and darkest in our sprout repertoire. They contain lots of natural black dye and because they take
the longest to grow, the water has more time to dissolve their black
pigment. Unlike the skin tight hulls of alfalfa, these seeds have large
husks. Like paint on wood, the twice daily rinsing eventually washes
off the dye.

The verdict, NOT GUILTY: Let the big sprouts go free. The con-
sensus: although the damage was unsightly, it did not interfere with
the normal growth and enjoyment of sprouts. Two techniques, however, are recommended for dealing with the blemished sprouters.
Soak the stained bamboo in a dilute mixture of Clorox and water (½
cup per gallon water) for several hours or until clean. Rinse the
bleached baskets thoroughly and air them out in the sun or a warm
oven. Once dry, there should be no Clorox odor. Repeat rinsing if
necessary. A more ecological alternative is hydrogen peroxide.
Immerse your baskets in full strength, 35% food grade hydrogen
peroxide. Let sit overnight. Because of its higher cost, strain the
H2O2 and recycle it for future use.

. Between the two bleaches, Clorox is stronger, yields cleaner baskets and is more economical. H2O2, although more expensive, is
completely non-toxic to people and the environment and has no
residual odor. Both work by oxidation. Use a deep bucket or basin
for complete immersion. If your baskets float, use a stone to hold
them down. Both sterilize and renew the baskets without harming
them.

Cleaning & Brightening Your Baskets

Cleaning and periodic sterilization of your baskets is necessary to
prevent mold and mildew and is recommended whenever the baskets appear dark and gray. It can be done sooner if your basket
shows severe discoloration or dark spots. Discoloration results from
the build-up of natural dyes leached from the hulls of the seeds.
Although completely harmless, they may be unsightly. Dark spots on
the other hand, are the result of mold and mildew which can

threaten the health of your crop. The spots are stains which are hard to remove unless bleached, but the molds themselves are actually very easy to remove and are normally flushed away during rinsing. Good, thorough rinsings prevents the buildup of mold spores and mildew. If these spots are a recurrent problem, it indicates insufficient rinsing or rinsing with too little water pressure. Inadequate air circulation in the greenhouse and/or temperatures too high also contributes to the problem. If your baskets are starting to show mold, brush them thoroughly under running water, even with sprouts still in them. If necessary, you may sterilize the basket by placing it in boiling water for about five minutes. This kills all germs and even whitens the bamboo a little. If dark spots still remain, you can remove them and brighten the basket by soaking it in a dilution of Clorox. Add ½ cup of Clorox to 1 gallon of water and let sit for one hour or more. When done, rinse well and let air dry. Because Clorox is a volatile liquid, it turns into gas quickly and escapes into the air. You can be sure that there is no Clorox residue in your baskets if there is no Clorox smell. The heat of the sun or a steady breeze will eliminate all traces of Clorox. Repeat this process of soaking and air drying a second time if any smell remains and use a more dilute solution next time. Clorox also sterilizes and can be used as a substitute for boiling. The longer you let your baskets sit in the solution, the more effective the bleaching. Slightly more bleach will give you quicker results. For a more ecological alternative to bleach, use hydrogen peroxide as a natural bleach and a preventative. *(See p. 53.)* The bamboo itself holds up surprisingly well to all this rinsing, boiling, and cleaning. The fiber itself never breaks down.

Sprouts like to snuggle inside the weave of the baskets just like they would weave and bury themselves into the earth. It is great for them, but may be a headache for you. Here is the trick to cleaning them out. Wash your baskets with water and a vegetable or scrub brush. Then put them aside and let dry. Do not try to wash out every sprout. Give a general washing with the vegetable brush, then dry the baskets in the sun or other warm spot. When the baskets are bone dry, brush them again with a bone dry brush. The dried sprouts easily flake off. Whatever you do, do not attempt perfection.

*Use a dry vegetable brush to eliminate the dry roots
from the basket weave or colander.*

There are thousands of roots and only one of you! Even with
your best efforts, you are still outnumbered. Instead, play the waiting
game; brush your baskets clean when the roots are dry and brittle.

Hydroponic Vs. Soil Grown

Hydroponics involves the growing of plants without soil. Nutrients
come from the water supply or, in commercial operations, through
synthetic fertilizers added as liquid food. Our method uses only
water as the source of nourishment for the growing plant, so it is of
primary importance that the water source is pure. Liquid kelp, available in natural food stores, can be added as additional plant food
and a natural fertilizer. Add the kelp first during soaking and once
more approximately halfway through the growth cycle. Put the
diluted kelp solution in a bowl and place the basket of sprouts in it.

The roots will soak up the nutrients from the solution. Sprouts grown with the aid of this liquid vitamin-drink taste sweeter. *(For more on liquid kelp, see p. 155.)*

Generally, plants grown in a non-soil environment are less nutritious than those grown in healthy soil. But because these seeds are so rich to begin with and soil on commercial farms today is so poor, these hydroponic sprouts are still far healthier than commercial vegetables. However, if you wish the maximum nutrition possible, and are willing to invest the time, grow all sprouts in organic soil.

A plastic greenhouse as designed by Sproutman. The lid would normally be closed. Greenhouses maintain temperature and moisture. Without them, seedlings would dry out and spoil.

The Flax Sprout Bag as designed by Sproutman.
Sweet pea sprouts are growing out of the top. On the bottom, from left
to right, are lentil, adzuki and mung beans.

Growing
GRAINS & BEANS
How to Use A Sprout Bag

Why A Sprout Bag

Sprout bags are a relatively new concept in sprouting. Although jars have been synonymous with sprouting since its inception, the advent of the sprout bag is revolutionizing sprouting. Bags have many advantages over jars. Sprout bags save time, space and hassle. Say goodbye to rubberbands, special lids, musty cheesecloth, angled jar racks and broken glass. Just immerse the bag in water, then hang it on a hook or knob, a faucet or just lay them in the dish rack. Where jars only breathe through a relatively small mouth, sprout bags yield perfect drainage and aeration on their entire surface. Fungus and growth problems occur because of too little air and too much moisture. Even your refrigerator will be happier when you remove all those bulky jars and replace them with sprout bags. They take up less space the more you eat. And don't leave home without one. Sprout bags are easy travelers. Take them with you on your next trip. They pack into lunch boxes, hang happily from your backpack, like long boatrides and enjoy the branch of a shady tree. Unlike jars, they never break.

About the Material

Sprout bags can be made of nylon, cotton, hemp or linen. Nylon is a strong material but is disappointing because it dries rapidly damaging the sprouts along the perimeter. Nylon is also a highly processed, synthetic fiber that is disturbing to many health conscious consumers even though there is little concern of chemicals leaching into the food. Cotton, on the other hand, is a highly sprayed crop and an excessively processed fiber. But the real problem with cotton is its pore openings which shrink and starve the sprouts blocking water drainage and air circulation. Burlap, which comes from the jute plant is too weak and unable to remain wet. It rots and unravels. Hemp is an exciting fiber with dozens of uses. However, until it is removed from the black-list of forbidden plants, it is too scarce and expensive to be practical. Crude linen is the most successful fiber for sprouting and is the least adulterated, too. Actually a product of the fibers from the flax plant, linen has been used for hundreds of years for clothing and tablecloths. It is known for its strength its high moisture absorbency and, in fact, is 20% stronger wet than dry. Linen sprout bags drain perfectly, maintain their coolness and are resistant to tearing. The flax fiber, or linen, never fluffs or frays and actually improves with laundering. A special honeycomb weave called huckaback ensures its durability making it ideal for sprouting.

SPROUT HISTORY LESSON

THE DARK AGES

The Jar

Description: Old fashioned method, cumbersome. Requires cheesecloth, screens, rubber bands. Cheesecloth collects bacteria.

Time: Time consuming 3-step process. Fill up, pour out, then tilt at an angle to store and drain.

Space: Takes up lots of shelf space and precious refrigerator space.

Air: Poor circulation. Air is limited by the narrow size of the opening.

Drainage: Incomplete. Mold created by stagnant water at bottom of jar.

Breakage: Requires extra care. Difficult to transport. Accidents ruin crop.

Size: Small jars overflow. Sprouts get little air. Hands can't get inside narrow opening. Takes up space.

Will Sprout: Sufficient for most beans and grains with some exceptions.

THE MODERN AGE

The Sprout Bag

Description: Made from the natural fibers of the Flax plant. Hand processed. No chemicals. Discovered by Sproutman circa 1979.

Time: Fast. Convenient 2 step action. Dip in water, hang on hook or knob.

Space: Bags expand or contract according to amount of growth and consumption.

Air: All sprouts get equal air. Good aeration prevents mold.

Drainage: Complete drainage without tilting or waiting. Good drainage prevents mold.

Durable: Actually 20% stronger wet than dry.

Portable: Lightweight, unbreakable. Great for traveling or camping.

Will Sprout: All nuts, grains, beans, legumes, vegetables, gelatinous seeds.

Advantages: Holds 3/4 gallon. Remains moist but not wet.

The Basics

1. *SOAK YOUR SEEDS IN A JAR OF PURE WATER OVERNIGHT.*
2. *POUR SOAKED SEEDS INTO PRE-MOISTENED SPROUT BAG. RINSE AND HANG BAG ON HOOK OR KNOB.*
3. *RINSE BAG SIMPLY BY IMMERSING IT IN WATER. RINSE TWICE PER DAY, NO MORE THAN 12 HOURS APART, FOR A MINIMUM OF 30 SECONDS.*

Wash Those Seeds!

Always examine your seeds for foreign debris and rinse them in cold water prior to soaking.

Preparing The Sprout Bag

Turn your sprout bag inside out and knot or cut off any loose hanging threads. Your sprout bag is hand sewn by dedicated sprout lovers. We are all perfect, but unraveling of the threads is natural with use. Soak your new bag thoroughly in warm water just prior to placing the pre-soaked seeds inside.

Soak your seeds in a 16-32 ounce jar with pure water.

Soaking the Seeds

Soak 1-2 cups of your favorite grains or beans in a jar of pure water for 8-12 hours or simply overnight. Fill a 16 or 32 ounce jar nearly to the top with pure water. If you want to boost your nutrition, add a few drops of liquid kelp *(optional, see p. 155)*. Then, pour the soaked seeds into the pre-moistened sprout bag. Do not soak the seeds inside the bag. Natural dye from the seed (and kelp) can stain the bag. Close the bag by pulling on the draw string. Dip the newly filled bag in pure, warm water and hang up to drain. Generally more grains fit in the bag than beans since they are smaller. A standard size sprout bag will soak up to 2½ cups of grains.

Rinsing

Rinse your sprouts twice daily, no more than 12 hours apart, by immersing the bag into a pot, basin or sink full of pure water. Let it set for at least 30 seconds. You may use the same rinse water if you are working with more than one bag, but change the water as soon as it discolors or looks dirty. Two rinsings per day is all you need, but a third is beneficial in hot weather or when working with large beans such as soybean and chick pea. Thorough washing prevents mold and fungus growth. Be faithful to your sprouts. Don't miss a rinsing. If you cannot be home, refrigerate them in the bag until you return or...take them with you!

Soak the seeds in a glass jar for 8-12 hours. Pour the soaked seeds into a pre-moistoned sprout bag. Rinse and hang.

The Sprout Massage

As the sprouts grow, they can send their roots into the weave of the sprout bag. This causes clumping and can weaken the bag wall. The solution: Give your sprouts a sprout massage! Grab the bag by the ends while under water and jiggle and swish it around moving the seeds freely inside the bag. C'est toute!

The Art of Draining

If there is an art to rinsing sprouts, then there is also an art to draining. Sprout bags are easy. Hang your sprout bag to drain on a hook or knob. Small hooks are easy to install and the sprout bag stops dripping after only a few minutes. If you find it inconvenient to hang, set the well drained bag on a dish, a dish rack or even a clean oven or dishwasher rack. Always keep your bag in a medium-to-warm spot and away from dry air or drafts which dry the bags out. Ideally, they should remain moist between rinsings.

Nature Does the Rest

Now, the sprouts are tucked away in their comfortable natural fiber home. Neither the grains nor the beans require darkness to grow, nor do they need light. Any light will do. Keep them in a neutral place that is convenient for you. Most beans will mature in 4 or 5 days while the grains take 2-4. Once mature, store them in the refrigerator and rinse once every second or third day. They will keep for one to two weeks.

Hang the sprout bag on a hook or a knob. Dripping stops after a few minutes.

How Much Seed?

A standard size 7x12 inch sprout bag sprouts 1-2½ cups of dry grains or beans. Because of the difference in the size of the seed, 1 cup of beans and 2 cups of grains is typical. Generally, sprouted grains and beans multiply 3 times their volume. As a rule, fill your bag to ⅓ capacity with dry seed leaving room for expansion.

Light

Neither grains nor beans require darkness to grow indoors. Keep them in a neutral spot that is convenient for you. If you choose to grow fenugreek, alfalfa or other chlorophyll developing sprouts in your sprout bag, spread the top of the bag open during the final sprouting days for exposure to light.

What Seeds To Sprout

Although sprout bags can sprout any seed, they are best suited for grains and beans.

Best Seeds for Growing in the Sprout Bag
Number of Days till Maturity

Easy		Advanced	
Lentil	[4-5]	Soybean	[4]
Adzuki	[4-5]	Hulled Sunflower	[2]
Mung	[4-5]	Peanut	[7]
Green Pea	[4-5]	Garbanzo	[4]
Hard Wheat	[2-3]	Chia	[12]
Soft Wheat	[2-3]	Flax	[2]
Rye	[2-3]	Triticale	[2-3]
Kamut	[3-4]		
Red Pea	[4-5]		
Fenugreek	[5-7]		

The "easy" list above represents the most popular and easiest sprouting seeds. Adzukis originally come from Asia. The domestic version is called the red pea. For sunflower, use the shelled "silver" version. Avoid all roasted and salted nuts, seeds, grains and beans. Nuts, in general, are not recommended for sprouting. Nuts can only be sprouted in their shells. Some varieties, almonds for example, have an outer shell which consumers never see. In all cases, the original shell must be intact with no sterilization or cleaning as is common with popular varieties such as walnuts. Even then, nuts can

take weeks to germinate and the results are not very satisfying. Keep
in mind, that nuts sprout into trees and that takes a long, long time.
Peanuts, by the way, are actually peas--part of the legume family.
Sunflower and pumpkin are seeds from the hearts of vegetables.
Hulled sunflower seeds can be sprouted for 2-3 days in the sprout
bag or a jar for a delicious snack. *(For growing sunflowers in the
shell, see p. 146.)* Pumpkin seeds, however, are disappointingly
bitter.

Large beans such as lima,
navy, kidney, black bean, etc.
are poor sprouters. Germination
of these beans is generally
between 40% and 60%. That
means that half the beans sprout
while the other half rot. The
bad beans infect the good beans
leaving you with a moldy mess.
Grocery store beans are especially poor sprouters because
many commercial brands are
scrubbed so clean they become

sterile. Big beans do better in a sprout bag than in a jar because of
the improved aeration and drainage. If you are going to sprout these
beans, they do better if rinsed more often than other sprouts. Rinse
3-4 times per day for best results.

Grains such as hard wheat, soft wheat, rye, triticale are good
sprouters. Rice, quinoa, oats, barley and millet, however, are a different story. Oats, barley and millet fall into a special group since they
cannot sprout in the popularly available form. These grains, as found
on your grocery shelves, are husked for cooking. The husk is a
heavy jacket that protects the seed. It is not just another fiber like
the bran in wheat. This fiber is a coarse ligneous cover that is
impossible to chew unless you are a horse. (Lignin is a woody cellulose.) Cooking does not help either. In order to sprout these varieties, you must obtain the agricultural, unhusked, whole seed which
you can only obtain from farm seed companies.

Rice, is another matter. Unless you have your own rice pattie, it is extremely difficult to sprout. Rice grows in marshy, flooded lands and has a long gestation period. This, plus its small shoot, makes it impractical for home sprouting. Quinoa can only grow with its saponin rich sheath (jacket) on and intact. Unfortunately, this is not how it comes when you purchase it at the health food store. *(See Quinoa, p. 77.)*

Alfalfa, radish, clover, fenugreek and other leafy green vegetable sprouts can grow in a sprout bag, but because of their desire for sunlight, you will get better results using a vertical sprouter. Sprout bags are so versatile, that they can even sprout the gelatinous seeds like chia, flax, psyllium, and cress *(see gelatinous seeds, p. 158)*. For information on long term storage of your grains and beans see *Storage, p. 69.*

Merry Mixtures

Why not mix? Grow a few varieties at once. It saves you time and effort. Most beans grow well together as long as their maturation times are similar. Try these proven combinations:

Combo A	*Combo B*	*Combo C*
¼ cup Mung	¼ cup Adzuki	¼ cup Mung
1 cup Lentil	1 cup Lentil	1 cup Lentil
		¼ cup Green pea

The Mother Bag Time Saver Method

Here is a simple time and space saving method when sprouting multiple varieties that cannot be grown in the same bag. Place one variety of bean in a large (mother) sprout bag. Place another in the regular size (baby) sprout bag. Insert the baby bag into the mother and sprout them together. This allows for multiple sprouting with one action. You can fit two babies inside one mother. Imagine, a mother that births twins in only 5 days! Massage the mother to keep the sprouts from rooting into the walls of the fabric. Your mother will be glad.

How To Clean A Sprout Bag

Empty your sprout bags and turn them inside out. Hose down the insides of the bag with a forceful spray of water from your dishwashing hose or faucet sprayer. In many cases, this is all that is necessary to clean your bag! Never use a brush, soap, or abrasives. Never use your bag to strain coffee or tea. They contain acids which dissolve the natural fiber.

☞ ☞ ☞ *NEVER USE SOAP, BLEACH, HYDROGEN PEROXIDE, OR A BRUSH AS IT WEAKENS THE NATURAL FIBERS.* ☜ ☜ ☜

Some of the bigger beans such as peanut, soy and chick pea can benefit from three rinsings per day. This is especially warranted in hot climates. When the wash water becomes cloudy, change it before washing the next variety. Whenever you see cloudy water, it is an indication to rinse more often or more thoroughly. Sterilize the bags by boiling after such a batch and whenever sprouts turn bad. Place the bags in a pot of boiled water for 3 minutes. Let the hot sprout bag hang dry in the inside out position. Wash by hand only. Never use bleach, hydrogen peroxide, soap, detergents or a brush as it weakens the natural fabric. Any sprout hulls or roots that remain in the bags can be shaken off easily once they are fully dry.

When To Sterilize Your Sprout Bag

✔ Sprouts smell sour
✔ Sprouts show signs of decay
✔ Presence of mold
✔ Cloudy water during rinsing

For longest life, do not handle the bag when it is dry and brittle. The flax fiber is brittle when dry and durable when wet. In fact, a wet bag is 20% stronger than a dry one. Always manipulate your bags when they are wet. This includes opening and closing the drawstring and turning the bag inside out for cleaning, etc. Wet the bag first, then turn it inside out, add seeds, etc. Some discoloration from the seeds is normal. Darkened bags will bleach and lighten slightly in the sun.

Avoid letting the rootlets hook into the bag. Here's how: wash your sprout bag by immersing it in a sink full of water or in a big pot. A sink has enough room in which to swish and jiggle the bag around. The flow of water through the bag better cleans the seeds. Because the seeds move around inside the bag, they are never in the same place long enough to root into the side walls. This makes cleaning easier and extends the life of your bag.

☞ ☞ ☞ A DRY FLAX BAG IS BRITTLE.
ALWAYS MANIPULATE YOUR SPROUT BAG WHEN WET.
A WET BAG IS 20% STRONGER THAN WHEN DRY. ☜ ☜ ☜

The Sprout Bag for Gelatinous Seeds

Gelatinous seeds are those that form a gel upon soaking. The most common ones for sprouting are chia, flax, cress and psyllium. These seeds cannot be sprouted using a jar, but they will sprout on top of a sprout bag. That's right--on top of, not inside the bag. Lay the bag out flat on a dish or a tray and sprinkle a single layer of seed on top of

**Gelatinous sprouts like chia
vertically grow on the outside
of a sprout bag, not inside.**

the bag covering it fully. Thoroughly spray the seeds and bag using a plant mister or atomizer. Mist again 5 minutes later. Keep vigilant the first 2 days to make sure the seeds do not dry out. Mist again if necessary. If you cannot keep watch, insert the growing sprouts in a greenhouse tent or firm plastic bag to maintain moisture. Mist twice daily and keep in a neutral spot. In approximately 9 to 14 days, your crop will mature and stand 3/4 to 2 inches tall depending on the variety. Pluck carefully and use in salads. Chia is sharp, flax is bitter, cress is hot and psyllium is mild. Store the sprout bag inside a plastic bag in the refrigerator for approximately one week.

Other Uses For Your Sprout Bag

Use your large "Mother" sprout bags for storing salad greens, extra sprouts and all vegetables. They work much better than plastic bags since they have excellent aeration and drainage yet remain moist. The bags themselves last for years.

You may also use your sprout bag to make both regular and non-dairy cheeses. They work better than cheese cloth. Just set the curds in the bag and hang. They're perfect for making soft cheeses like ricotta, farmer and cottage cheese. For non-dairy cheeses made from cashew and sunflower, hang in a warm spot to aid the natural enzymes in curing the cheese. *(For more read Sproutman's Kitchen Garden Cookbook, see p. 193.)* *Caution:* Natural enzymes may be strong enough to digest the fiber of the bag itself. Be certain to thoroughly clean your bag of all food matter which can rot and weaken the fibers. Monitor your bag carefully so as to preserve it for years of sprouting use.

Sprouted Wheat and Fenugreek

AFTER

THEY'VE GROWN

Life Expectancy

With proper care, most home grown varieties last from one to two weeks after harvest. One of the most important steps in extending the life of your sprouts is cleaning them. Cleaning means washing away the hulls. Hulls are inert (dead) matter that decays and can ruin your crop if not removed. After harvesting, clean your sprouts well in order to get the most longevity from them. *(See p. 50.)*

HEALTHY, WELL CLEANED SPROUTS, LAST FROM ONE TO TWO WEEKS IN THE REFRIGERATOR.

Refrigeration

The need to refrigerate your sprouts depends on these factors:

  a) Their age and condition
  b) Temperature or season
  c) Quantity available vs. capacity to consume

If your sprouts are old or in poor condition, you must refrigerate them. Sprouts are at their prime during harvest time (approximately one week old). They will generally survive as long as it took for them to mature. This means if cabbage takes five days to mature, you will have at least another five--plus days in which to eat them. If alfalfa takes seven days to mature, it will survive for another week or more, and so on. Refrigeration would also be beneficial in a situation where you just have too many sprouts--more than you could finish in the time left before they would naturally go bad.

Refrigeration does not stop a sprout's growth, it just slows it down. You be the judge and make your decision based on your needs and the needs of your crop.

Once mature, you will have to refrigerate your sprouts for at least part of the time. How often depends on their condition. Identify an unhealthy sprout by its...

> a) Bad odor
> b) Soft or soggy spots
> c) Drying or darkening of roots
> d) Darkening or losing color

Bad odor is the first sign that sprouts are aging. You will smell a problem before you will see it. Texture is the next clue. Young sprouts are firm when fresh. Older sprouts will develop areas that are soft or soggy. Examine the underside of the basket where the root system comes through and you will see how the roots show signs of deterioration long before the tops. The roots may look brown or dried out. Eventually the tops will tend to lose their richness of color and darken, too. If you see any of these signs, the sprouts must be refrigerated.

Since refrigeration is always recommended after maturity, it is only a question of how long to keep them refrigerated. Basically, there are three choices. You can 1) refrigerate them full time, 2) nights only, or 3) most of the time, taking them out for only a few hours per day. It is usually necessary to refrigerate sprouts full time in the hot weather. In milder weather, you can keep your sprouts out for a few hours in the afternoon to allow them to green up. Or, if the day is too hot, place them out in the evening under Vita-lites. This will help them green up. In winter or cooler weather, you can keep them out all day and just refrigerate them at night.

Rinsing When Stored in the Refrigerator

Sprouts get by with fewer rinsings in the refrigerator. You may choose to rinse once a day, once every other day, or once every third day, depending on 1) their general condition, 2) the humidity of your refrigerator, and 3) the temperature of your refrigerator.

First evaluate your needs based on the three factors--age, temperature, and amount--then examine your sprouts for the 4 aspects of their condition--odor, texture, moisture and color. The less favorable the factors and the worse the condition, the more you need to refrigerate. Next, keep in mind that some refrigerators, like the ones that are frost-free, are very dry and could require you to rinse your sprouts once every day or two. If your refrigerator is not frost free and is sufficiently humid, you may rinse every second or third day. But the best way to insure proper storage is in the greenhouse tent. In this way they can store the longest between rinsings and are the least vulnerable to refrigerator variations. On the average, you can be safe rinsing once every other day. One caution: keep your sprouts away from the freezer section, since sprouts are delicate and very susceptible to frost. Even the healthiest sprouts cannot survive a frost.

If your refrigerator is overcrowded with no space for a basket, pull your sprouts out, clean them, and stuff them in a sprout bag, a glass jar or plastic container. Plastic bags are unfit for storing sprouts because they suffocate a live plant.

Some sprouts are just endowed with a heartier constitution than others and last longer. Of the group, alfalfa, fenugreek and turnip will last the longest. Red clover, cabbage, mustard and radish are the weaker set, and need more attention and care.

Refrigerator Storage

*USE THIS METHOD ONLY FOR STORAGE IN THE REFRIGERA-
TOR. OR, HARVEST AND PLACE SPROUTS IN A GLASS
OR PLASTIC CONTAINER.*

Remember, sprouts will not survive as long in the hot weather. They suffer from a condition known as root rot, something similar to athlete's foot. The treatment: keep them cool and clean.

About Light

All of the green leafy sprouts that we have been discussing require light to develop chlorophyll and achieve their peak nutrition. That is why they are called "heliotropic"--sun finders. The concept behind the basket or vertical sprouter is that it allows for a large surface area where sprouts rise straight up to the sun. These seeds are, to repeat, alfalfa, red clover, fenugreek, radish, cabbage, turnip, kale, mustard, whole sunflower, buckwheat, wheatgrass, chia, cress, and psyllium.

True, all seeds need some light. But if you are a gardener, you know that some vegetables do better in shade, that is, indirect light. Therefore, we need to define light as direct and indirect. Direct, hot light is ideal for many vegetables, but indirect is better for all sprouts. Sprouts that get direct sunlight tend to cook, and even if you let them cook for only an hour or two, you may ruin your entire crop. Sprouts must remain cool. Vegetables which have their roots in soil can keep themselves cool and constantly in contact with moisture. Sprouts, on the other hand, have no means of dissipating their heat and rely on you to supply them with water. In addition, the greenhouse tents used to keep our soil-free indoor crop moist, retain the heat that penetrates it. Therefore, greening is best done with indirect light or shade. These sprouts, surprisingly, need very little light to achieve their full chlorophyll development.

Actually, the little sprout is not even able to utilize light for the first 3 or 4 days of its life. This means that alfalfa, which takes seven days to mature, only needs light for the last half of its growing period. Darkness, however, is not necessary at any point. The old tale of keeping your sprouts in a dark closet in order to germinate them, is really not required. The germination of seeds in darkness really applies to long term vegetables grown in soil. In this case, darkness affords a longer germination period and emboldens the seed for the long term growth. Some vegetables take 150 days to mature. Sprouting seeds mature in 7 to 14 days. For this reason, darkness is of little consequence. Simply allow indirect light or shade from beginning to end and your sprouts will be happy.

Like many good things, sun is both a provider and an enemy. In winter, sunlight keeps sprouts warm and keeps them growing at a normal rate. Sprouts grow more slowly in the winter because of the cold. During this time, it is to your advantage to carefully add some more direct sunlight to your indoor crop. Your main concern is to protect the sprouts from overheating. Remember, the greenhouse retains the heat that penetrates it. This, in addition to the heat produced from the sprouts own organic growing process, may become too much for the struggling seeds to withstand. Test your crop by opening the greenhouse tent and putting your hand inside. Your hand acts as a human thermometer. You are now taking the sprouts temperature. The ideal temperature for a sprout is between 65 and 75 degrees. But on a hot day when the room temperature is 85 degrees, the temperature in the greenhouse may be 10-20 degrees higher. Sprouts can survive brief periods of high temperatures for short periods, but it is not ideal. During the warm weather, take your sprouts temperature often and if they are too warm, put them in a cooler spot and do not forget to rinse. One of the main reasons for rinsing is to cool the sprouts down. Be sure to use absolutely cold rinse water in the summer and don't be shy about giving your sprouts one extra rinse each day.

Curiously, Winter sprouting also involves the danger of overheating from your radiator! Most heat radiators are near windows and window sills are usually where sprouts are set. Be careful. As an indoor gardener, it is your responsibility to control the growing environment, just like the gardener out of doors has to know when it is the best time to plant certain seeds. So don't radiate your sprouts. Keep them between 65 and 70 degrees, keep them in the shade, and create as stable an environment as possible.

Cleaning Seed Hulls

The hull is the dark colored jacket which covers all the seeds. As the sprout germinates, the jacket eventually falls off from the action of the sprout's growth and the rinsings which soften and loosen the hull. In this respect, the sprouts clean their own hulls. The problem with hulls is that they all lay at the bottom of the sprouter and inevitably become a part of our salad. True, hulls are not poison, nor are they always undesirable. They are to sprouts like bran is to wheat: fibrous shells that clothe the seed. For the most part, these hulls, like bran, are simply indigestible roughage. In some cases, the hulls bind certain minerals such as calcium and phosphorous and make it harder to utilize these minerals. But mostly, the disadvantage of hulls is their unpalatability. It does not take advanced math to realize that there are as many hulls as there are sprouts and if you did not clean your hulls, your salads would have a lot of hulls. Unless you are a fiber fanatic, you will want to eat a salad comprised primarily of sprouts. So, it is important to find a convenient way to clean those hulls.

Timing is most important. Do not try to get the hulls off before they are ready to let go. The best time to clean the hulls is right after the first harvest. At this time, most of the sprouts have formed their leaf division. When the leaves divide, the sprouts throw off their softened hulls. They actually do the hulling, all we have to do now is the removal.

Immerse the entire basket in a basin of pure water. Agitate the basket or swish it from side to side. Notice how the hulls rise to the surface of the water. Quickly slide the basket out from under the floating hulls being careful not to take the hulls with you. That's all. If necessary, repeat for further cleaning. Another approach is to put the basket in the water face down. Be careful your sprouts are well rooted before trying this. If you are unsure, protect them with your hand as you immerse the basket. Once the sprouts are rooted, however, you can freely agitate the basket in an inverted position and the sprout will not fall out...only the hulls. Do not turn the basket upright under water. Lift it out of the water in the inverted position and watch the hulls fall straight into the water. Give a final brief rinse with your sink sprayer, then set the basket at an angle to drain. You will find this immersion--cleaning method the fastest and simplest. *(For cleaning the shells off Buckwheat and Sunflower sprouts see p. 149.)*

You can start using the inverted position as soon as your roots have anchored into the basket which, for most sprouts, will begin on the fourth day. Observe the underside of the basket to confirm that roots are established. If the roots are not weaving into the basket after four days, you are disturbing their orientation. During the first four days, the sprouts are busy extending roots and up righting themselves. Do not disturb their organization when you rinse. Be thorough, rinse with your spray hose forcefully but evenly, but keep them relatively in the same position. If sprouts could speak they would hang a sign reading, *"Sprouts At Work. Do Not Disturb."*

Cleaning Sick Sprouts

Here is an alternate method for cleaning to be used on that rare chance occasion when your sprouts have gone bad. (Not possible after reading this book!) First, throw away those sprouts that appear limp, soggy, shriveled and dry, or have a sour odor. Next, pull out the remaining restorable ones and place them in a basin of pure water. Set the basin in the sink. Agitate the sprouts until they have separated. Fill the basin to the top with water and skim the hulls off the top. It is helpful to use a basin with a pour spout. As you fill the water up to the brim, the hulls will leave through the spout. When the water settles, grab no more than a handful of sprouts at a time, rinse then lay them in a fresh basket or colander to drain. Continue until you have gotten out all that you can grab. Pour the remaining sprouts into the basket making sure to stop before the sediment pours through. Sediment consists of 1%-2% seeds that do not sprout and of hulls that sink rather than float. This method, which is the same one used to clean grains and beans grown in the sprout bag, can revive a sick crop or improve a healthy one. As you see, this involves more time than the immersion method *(see p. 17)*, so use it mainly to save a sick or aging batch of sprouts. Throw the soggy ones out and let the others continue to lead a clean life.

The inverted rinsing method provides regular cleaning of the hulls each time you rinse your sprouts. You will accomplish the most cleaning after the first harvest. But do not expect to wash away every hull. Do not work with a magnifying glass and don't take all day. Some people spend more time cleaning their sprouts than they do themselves! Don't become a slave to your sprouts. Sprouts are here to serve you.

Fear of Mold

Mold is the sprouters nemesis. Fear of mold is enough to keep an aspiring sprouter from getting started. Did you know that mold, mildew, yeast, bacteria, mushrooms and rust are all plants? Unlike green plants, this group, known as fungi, has neither roots nor

leaves and cannot manufacture its own food. Instead, they are parasites feeding on other plants and dead organic matter. Fungi spores
are omnipresent in nature and arrive along with your seed. Sprouting seed should be carefully selected for low fungi counts. Like any
plant, fungi need time to grow. Your job as a sproutarian is to wash
them away before they mature. Since they do not have roots, fungi
sit on the backs of your seeds. Flooding your sprouts with good,
strong water pressure washes them off the sprouts and down the
drain. If you do not wash well, fungi will reproduce sending out fila-
ments which anchor them in place. The first few days of washing are
critical. A dish sprayer hose or faucet spray adaptor are required for
proper washing. Wash the basket walls, rims and underside as well.
If you see a white fuzz developing on the growing seeds, that is
your indication that you need to rinse longer or with greater water
pressure. The white mold is not harmful and easily rinses off. If a
gray or darker mold occurs, discard the batch, sterilize your
sprouter and start again. Lapse time between rinsings should be no
more than 12 hours. Temperatures of 70-78 degrees F. are ideal.
Higher temperatures may require more frequent rinsings to cool the
sprouts. If a gray or dark mold occurs, discard the batch, sterilize
your sprouter and start again. If mold clings to the bamboo walls,
brush the area clean under running water. As the sprouts grow,
eliminate the hulls with the inversion method of rinsing described
on *p. 17.* Seed hulls are dead matter that provide a breeding
ground for mold.

Hydrogen Peroxide For Prevention of Mold

As surprising as it may sound, Hydrogen Peroxide, similar to the
kind that sits on drug store shelves across America, has become a
rising star as a healing agent in alternative therapies for degenerative diseases including even AIDS and cancer.

What is Hydrogen Peroxide? $H_2O_2 = H_2O + O$, or...water plus an
extra oxygen molecule. Water and oxygen are the two most vital elements of life, but how does it fight disease? Therapeutically, the
extra oxygen is used to increase the overall oxygen level in the

blood. This hyper-oxygenation is wonderful for normal cells and strengthens the immune system. But cancer cells, by their nature, are anaerobic and oxidize (combust) in an elevated oxygen environment.

Alternative health clinics in Mexico and West Germany have been using bio-oxidative therapies with impressive results and many individuals tell of its success in treating arthritis, candida, herpes and other ailments including the common cold.

How does this relate to sprouts? Mold growth is inhibited with the use of Hydrogen Peroxide. When added to the soak water or the rinse water, mold development can be reduced or eliminated entirely and the extra oxygen encourages a more robust crop. It is this oxygen that burns or "combusts" the mold.

Pharmaceutical brands of peroxide have numerous additives, stabilizers and buffers to keep the oxygen from escaping as well as a low 3% potency. Even so, it is effective in destroying germs and is the best mouthwash. Food grade peroxide is 35% potent and 100% pure. Only 15 drops are necessary to add to your soak or rinse water. Let the rinse water sit for at least 5 minutes. The treatment need not be applied every rinse but only when necessary or once every 2 days as regular maintenance. It is an aid and a preventative, but not a necessity. *(To obtain food grade peroxide, see resources, p. 180.)* If you are interested in the therapeutic use of oxygen, the book, *Oxygen Therapies* by Ed McCabe, is also an excellent resource on the different bio-oxidative treatments, uses, clinics, and background information. *(See p. 180.)*

How To Apply H2O2 On Sprouts

Cautions on Handling H2O2. Full strength (35%) Hydrogen Peroxide (H2O2) can cause temporary white spots on the skin with burning and itching. Use rubber gloves whenever handling full strength H2O2. Rinse the exterior of the bottle with water before and after using. As with all medicines and chemicals, keep out of reach of children. Full strength H2O2 is not for human consumption. Always dilute before using. Avoid contact with eyes. Handle with care.

Method [1] Soaking the Seeds. Add ½ teaspoon of full strength (35%) H2O2 to the water in which you soak your seeds. Use 16oz of soak water. The H2O2 helps disinfect any bacteria in the seeds and increases the amount of available oxygen and nitrogen to them. Expect some seeds to rise and bubbles to form.

Method [2] Misting the Sprouts. Use the same dilution of ½ teaspoon of H2O2 in a pint (16oz) of water. Spray the sprouts with a mister bottle once or twice per day for extra oxygenation and disinfection. Spray the sides and bottoms of the basket, too! Misting with 2O2 does not replace regular twice daily rinsings with plain water. Use H2O2 *after* rinsing with water. Caution: Stronger solutions may burn the delicate tips of leafy sprouts such as alfalfa and buckwheat turning them brown or yellow.

Method [3] Soaking the Sprouts in a Basin. Soak your basket sprouters in a basin or sink full of water. Treat the water in the sink with the equivalent of a ½ teaspoon per 16oz of water. This is just enough to hear a light fizz when listening to the baskets. This helps generally oxygenate the sprouts and keeps them free of mold.

Method [4] Treating the Baskets. Pour full strength 35% H2O2 into a large pot with a lid and immerse your baskets in the solution. Let sit for 4-8 hours, then strain and recycle the H2O2 back into its original bottle. This treatment, for new or old baskets, sterilizes the baskets and makes them resistant to mold.

Treating Grains and Beans. Because they do not have delicate green leaves, grains and beans, like wheat, garbanzos, peanuts, soybeans, etc., may be soaked in a stronger dilution of H_2O_2. Use 1 tsp per 16 ounces of water. Caution: Do not soak your sprout bag in H_2O_2. Its natural fibers will be weakened by the oxidizing action of the peroxide.

Mold Discoloration. If mold does develop, it can create black or dark spots on your baskets. Used early, H_2O_2 will prevent the development of mold and thus its discoloration. Although H_2O_2 stops mold, the 35% concentration may not be strong enough to bleach out all the dark stains. Bad stains can be removed with another strong oxidizer, Clorox bleach. Mix a 1 to 1 Clorox to water solution and submerge the stained basket. Let soak until bleached clean. Bleach is not as environmentally desirable as H_2O_2.

Growing Wheatgrass in Soil. When growing wheatgrass in soil, mold can develop on the soil surface. Using a mister bottle, spray the surface with a 1 teaspoon per 16oz H_2O_2 dilution. A loose soil mixture of 50% peat moss and top soil is helpful.

Care for House Plants. H_2O_2 can help eliminate mold buildup on clay plant pots and saucers and control the infestation of some small insects which attack plant foliage. Spray on 1 teaspoon per 16oz of water. Stronger dilutions may be acceptable depending on the hardiness of the plant. For spraying directly on leaves, test the concentration first on a small area.

Natural Elimination of Mold. Mold is a fungus which thrives in moist environments and poor ventilation. Like all micro-organisms, it needs time to develop. Regular rinsing with strong water pressure mechanically removes the mold bacteria before they can take hold. The best prevention of mold problems is the daily rinsing of your sprouts with good water pressure. H_2O_2 is not a substitute for rinsing.

SEEDS

Biogenic means life-generating. Biogenic foods are germinated seeds, whole grains, nuts, legumes, and tender baby greens which have the biochemical capacity to mobilize their dormant life forces and thus create and generate new life.

SEED PERSONALITIES
Their Tastes and Growing Times

Seeds are just as different as people. Some are easy, some are tough. Some are fast, some are slow. Know your seeds and your sprouting days will be healthier and happier. Here's a list of some of their characteristics with apologies to Mother nature.

Black Oil Sunflower. The biggest of the bunch. A towering blossom of health. Four percent protein--more than spinach! Takes approximately 10 days to mature. With the black oil sprouting variety, 99% of the shells fall off naturally. Has a tremendous appetite for water. The shells themselves (not the seeds) are prone to fungus. Rinse thoroughly twice per day (don't miss) with plenty of water pressure and leave plenty of air in the greenhouse tent. Remove them with a fork and flush the area clean. Sunflower--can you guess--likes the sun. Just make sure they do not get too hot. Plenty of rinsing cools them and helps the shells slip off. Basket method.

Radish. Watch out. This is a hot one and can bite! Respect your radish and it will provide many happy meals for you. Takes 5-6 days to mature. Shells fall off easily. A white fur is common to see growing during early growth. This indicates watering is not adequate either in terms of pressure, volume or frequency. The white fur is harmless and easily rinsed away. Don't let it go too far or it could lead to mold. China Rose Radish is the best sprouting variety. It has beautiful colored leaves and red stalks. Radish will clear clogged sinuses and chest. Great to mix with milder varieties. Basket method.

Cabbage. A little guy with a light green complexion and a notch at the top of the head. Takes 5 days to mature. Because of its small size, Cabbage finds it more difficult to root into the basket weaves than other sprouts. Try not to disturb the seeds' orientation during days 2-4. This is the critical period when it attempts to root. Once they root, they are rather tight fisted and unlike the others, need to be yanked out in lumps. Lots of seeds remain on the bottom. The seed jackets can mold, so rinse them out and rinse the harvested sprouts as well. Basket method.

Turnip, rutabaga, kale, and *rapeseed* are exotic members of the cabbage family. *Black mustard* looks like the cabbage family but is much hotter. These are delicious sprouts especially if you like cabbage, but they are hard to find. 5-6 days maturity. Basket method.

Alfalfa. The most famous sprout and a celebrity to whom all others owe a debt of gratitude. Alfalfa gets its name from the Arabic "alf-al-fa," father of all foods. One of the richest sources of chlorophyll and magnesium as witnessed by its dark green color. Mild tasting. It holds on to its seed jackets tightly and matures in 7 days when 90% of them have fallen. Rinsing in the inverted position *(see p. 17)* successfully eliminates most hulls. Sensitive to hot temperatures and direct sunshine. Alfalfa will decay if it gets too hot indicated by a softening (mushiness) of the stalk and an ammonia smell. Avoid this during hot weather by rinsing more often and with cold water. Keep in a shady spot. Basket method.

Red Clover. A cousin of alfalfa, considers itself the prettiest of all sprouts and whether or not you agree, it is certainly one of the fastest and easiest to grow. It matures in only 6 days. Although it is not quite as tall as Alfalfa, it has a sharper flavor, a larger leaf, and a lighter green complexion. It surrenders its hulls easily making it the simplest of sprouts to clean. Don't miss this grand lady. Basket method.

Crimson Clover. There are many kinds of clover but crimson has the largest leaf. A cousin of alfalfa, it has all the same characteristics especially regarding hot temperature. It is even more sensitive to heat than alfalfa. It relieves its seed jackets or hulls readily--more than any other seed, providing a clean, green salad free of hulls. This clover is related to the famous 4-leaf clover and other clovers blooming on your lawn in the spring. Basket method.

Buckwheat. Buckwheat is actually not a wheat at all but an herb, which is good news to those of you with wheat allergies. It is quite big--4-5 inches tall and rich in B-vitamin factors like choline and inositol. Buckwheat takes approximately 10 days to mature and is ready when 90% of its hulls have fallen off. You'll never get 100% hull removal so don't try because the seeds ripen at different rates. Harvest by yanking out a 1 inch handful and either washing or cutting off the hulls at the roots. Because the hulls are so large, they can develop fungus. Take special care washing the buckwheat seeds during the rooting stage (first 5-6 days). Good thorough washing of the seeds and the baskets eliminates mold. Buckwheat needs light, warmth and moisture in order to maximize hull drop-off. Basket method. *(For more on buckwheat see p. 146.)*

Garlic & Onion Chives. The healthiest form of these vegetables is the young plant. These healing foods are easier to digest and rich in chlorophyll at this early stage of their development and they possess all the mysterious cell factors that make these foods famous in folklore and herbal medicine. Chlorophyll neutralizes the famous odor. The young chives take 14 days to mature. The black seed jackets hang on tenaciously. Surrender to them, they are okay to eat. Be patient. You may not see any sign of growth for 7 days. This is normal. Garlic and onion resist all fungus growth--wouldn't you know it! Basket method.

China Red Pea. This bean makes pea greens 4-6 inches tall! Lots of fiber in the stalks, mild taste. Take care to let the roots anchor in the basket. As your crop matures, wash away fallen bean husks and seed matter which are prone to decay. Cousin of mung. Matures in 8-10 days. Can also be sprouted in bag for 3-4 days. More on this bean later.

Kamut Egyptian Wheat. A high protein (18%), big brother of American wheat (12%). It's delicious. Takes 3-4 days in the sprout bag for the shoots to grow to half the size of the berry. This is the right length for making a delicious sprout bread. Shake the grains within the bag to keep them from rooting into the fabric walls. *(See Kamut, p. 75.)*

Soft White Wheat. This whole grain has no relation to white flour. The term "white" refers to its golden color. This grain has less protien and gluten than regular wheat and is used for pastry flour in the baking trade. Sprout it in the sprout bag for two days to make sprout crackers and cookies or 3-4 days for snacks. Great mixed with raisins.

Shelled "Silver" Sunflower. This is the standard sunflower with the shell removed. Grow this sunflower in the sprout bag for only 2 days. Because there is no shell cover, the air will oxidize the seeds turning them brown in color much like a half-eaten apple turns brown after a minute. There is no harm. Refrigerate the sprout after 2 days growth. Enjoy in salads or as a snack. Great with raisins.

Lentil & Green Pea. Easy to grow beans taking 5 days in the sprout bag. The pea is still a raw bean and needs cooking or steaming for consumption in any volume.

Sproutable Barley. This is a special hybrid variety of barley that is grown without the usual heavy husk on it. Often, when the husk is removed, the germination is damaged and may be as low as 80%. You can use barley for making sprout bread just like wheat. Sprouted barley is famous for making *barley malt*, the sweetener developed as the sprout converts its starch into grain sugar (maltose). The bread is delicious and "meaty" and can serve as a vegetarian "meat loaf" substitute. Since we cannot eat whole barley because of its heavy husk, this barley is a welcome alternative. However, it is rare and hard to find. Sprout bag.

Mung & Adzuki. These small beans take only 5 days to grow in the sprout bag. They are Chinese cousins. Mung requires a little extra work removing the seed jackets although the jackets are harmless and a good source of fiber. Empty your mung into a sink or pot full of water and skim off the green hulls as they float to the top. Mung is also famous for an occasional hard seed which won't sprout and, regrettably, feels like a pebble in your mouth. Sprout bag.

Fenugreek. One of the tallest and greenest sprouts. A bitter herb. For best flavor, always mix with alfalfa and clover. Fenugreek is easy to grow and mature in 8-9 days. Excellent for soothing the digestive track. Does best in cool temperatures, below 75°. It blends excellently with the other sprouts. Basket or sprout bag.

Wheatgrass. Wheatgrass is the 12-14 day wheat sprout that resembles the grass in your backyard. The grass is not eaten in salads because it is too fibrous to swallow. Although cows and horses do a fine job on grass, humans don't have the stomach for it. Instead, the grass is grown for its juice. Soil method. *(More about wheatgrass on p.150.)*

Gelatinous Seeds. *Chia, Flax,* and *Psyllium* are all gelatinous seeds which create a small amount of pretty greens cherished more for their ornamental beauty than for their contribution to your salad. As a group, they mature in approximately two weeks (14 days) and are spicy, bitter and mild tasting respectively. *(For more on sprouting gelatinous seeds, see p. 157.)*

Growing Garlic & Onion

Garlic chives and French onion are very special seeds and they require a special sprouting effort. They are the most expensive seeds in our sprouting repertoire and also have the longest growth period--about two weeks. But they are also the most flavorful and among the most popular.

Worth The Wait? Most garlic/onion lovers say, *Yes!* The health value of these two herbs is widely proclaimed. Garlic's reputation is well documented in history. The history books are full of people wearing garlic to ward off evil spirits and treat the common cold. Onion was used to soothe a throbbing earache and heal a bruise. We have lost touch with these potent herbs and are just starting to rediscover their healing value. Now we have them bottled and encapsulated and we separate out the odor. Much advertising hype is heaped on the public by supplement manufacturers about their product and how it is more potent or more odor-free. But *nothing* is better than eating the fresh plant. All the elements of the mature garlic bulb are in the sprouts and baby garlic plants are even more concentrated.

The Sprouting Advantage. The young 14 day garlic/onion chive has all the food elements that make the bulb famous. In fact, at this early stage, the plant is manufacturing amino acids at a faster rate than at any other time in the plant's growth. Because it needs to synthesize protein for building cells, it is bursting with vitamins. Vitamins require minerals and minerals require trace minerals and all of them require enzymes. This active living organism is concentrated with the kind of nutrition that supports fundamental cell growth.

This "live" food has something the dried garlic bulb does not--chlorophyll. Chlorophyll is nature's breath freshener. Companies spend thousands of dollars in laboratories trying to rid garlic of its essential aroma. But nature has its own solution and you only get it when you eat the *whole* green garlic plant. This is the *sprout* advantage.

Two Sprouter Technique. Because garlic and onion take two weeks to mature, you will see little growth for the first seven days. The first week is the hatching period and the best way to hatch seed is in a warm sprout bag. Most sprouting seeds like to germinate at 75 degrees. When winter makes this impossible, the soaking and first 48 hours of germination should be in a warm spot. The result is a sprout that grows faster, is heartier and has a greater percentage of germinating seed. This is especially beneficial for garlic and onion. If you have a warm spot, perhaps in or on top of your oven, hatch your seeds there. After the seed has burst and the shoots are ¼ inch long, transplant them into the small 6 inch sprouter. It takes only 2 tablespoons of dry seed to make a lavish crop, making these seeds more economical than they appear. These natural antibiotics will purify your bloodstream, your liver, and fight germs and parasites. The odor lasts only minutes--not hours! Go garlic!

The China Red Pea

This common but unfamiliar legume is the American version of the Asian adzuki. It is also one of the best kept sprouting secrets. This bean, which is related to mung, is an excellent germinator and a versatile sprouter. It can be consumed just like mung or lentil, in Chinese style wok dishes, soups or salads. Like all beans, be sensitive to how much you can digest raw. It grows best in a sprout bag and matures in 4-5 days with a tail approximately one inch long. Unlike its cousin mung, it has no hard seeds.

Now, put away your sprout bag and take out your basket sprouter. We're going to grow *red pea greens*. Treat this bean just like buckwheat or sunflower. Start with 5 tablespoons of peas in your large 9 inch sprouter. It takes approximately 10 days to develop 7 inch long stalks with big, beautiful green leaves. Although similar to buckwheat lettuce in appearance, it is richer in cellulose which will keep you chewing longer. Harvesting is simple. Just grab a small handful midway down the stalk and wiggle free. The roots are clean and white and should be eaten. Sprouts offer us the rare opportunity to enjoy a whole vegetable including its roots. Although their flavor is not as delicate as buckwheat or as hardy as sunflower, pea greens are bigger than the latter and easier to grow and harvest.

Fennel

Fennel is a relative of dill and caraway, but unlike its cousins, it is a good germinator. It is a vertical growing seed that develops a delicate green shoot. Although they will also sprout in the sprout bag, a vertical sprouter provides the best growing environment for them .

Fennel is a slow-to-start seed with a harvest time of approximately 14 days. Unlike other sprouting seeds, there is no hull to fall off. Both seed and shoot can be eaten and enjoyed. And what flavor! Fennel is an aromatic herb that adds zest to any salad or grain dish. It can even be included in sprout bread. Fennel is easily digestible in the raw state and a small amount goes a long way because of its rich flavor. Soak 3 Tbsp overnight and germinate in a 6 inch basket or vertical sprouter for 10-14 days. Sprouts store in the refrigerator for approximately 1 week.

Gas Those Mung!

Why are store bought mung beans so white and fat? This is a question often asked by home sprouters who strive to duplicate what they see in the supermarket. The difference is *ethylene gas.*

Ethylene gas is a plant hormone that occurs naturally in fruits such as bananas, mangoes, pineapples, kiwi, papayas and even tomatoes. Next time you buy bananas green, place them in a closed paper bag. The natural ethylene gas will concentrate and ripen the fruit faster. Warm temperatures of 85°-90° increase the rate of ethylene production.

For many years, professional Chinese sprouters burned incense in order to create ethylene gas by burning up the oxygen and creating more carbon dioxide. They also placed heavy weights on the mung beans which, because of the pressure, increased the ethylene gas.

Although commercial growers today use gas machines, you can create your own gas. Place a ripening banana in a paper bag along with a sprout bag full of 2 day old mung sprouts. Use a green banana and allow it to turn yellow. Do not let the banana rot or it may rot your sprout bag. You may also place weights on the mung beans, by growing them vertically in a basket or collander. Use a 9 inch sprouter and after 2 days growth, place a weight on the surface. For weights, use a sprout bag filled with small stones. A paper or plastic bag will also work. The bag covers the sprouts evenly and allows air circulation. House the sprouter in the greenhouse tent as usual.

Getting Organic Seeds

A study taken in 1942 showed there was a 5%-8% crop loss due to pests. Because of the push for productivity during the war, that amount of loss was considered unacceptable, so pesticide use became widespread. By 1947, everybody used them. In 1987, the United States Dairy Association did a study and found that crop loss due to pests was about 7%. What have we accomplished?

The Federal Environmental Protection Agency classifies more than 70 of the currently licensed 360 pesticide ingredients as potential carcinogens. Over the years, the Government's report card on its role as consumer protector has generally been poor and the agri-business industry has been slow to regulate itself or incorporate non-chemical methods. Throughout the Reagan-Bush Administrations, government has sided with industry claiming the economic risks to manufacturers were greater than the health risks to consumers. Congress and the F.D.A. have been slow to act, but thanks to the scare from Alar on apples and the arsenic laden Chilean grapes, they have begun imposing stricter legislation on the control of pesticide residues in foods. A high level E.P.A. administrator was recently quoted saying "Pesticides dwarf the other environmental risks the agency deals with. Toxic waste dumps may affect thousands of people, but virtually everyone is exposed to pesticides." Our solution has always been--support organic farming and...grow your own sprouts! *(See pesticides, p. 129.)*

Truly Organic?

The word organic is getting very popular of late. In fact, this seven letter word can mean more money for members of the food industry. Because of this, there is the inevitable abuse. The only way to insure that your money is being spent on truly organic food is through third party certification. Organic farmer certification programs are being set up in most states by independent groups whose job it is to promote organic farming and to provide a means of standardization and verification. Such groups are New York Organic Farmers Association, Vermont Organic Farmers Association and Ohio Ecological Food & Farm Association to name a few *(see p. 180)*. A farmer must become a member of such a group. The group inspects the farm and informs the farmer what is required of him in order to comply. Some farms are certified while others are in transition and have their application pending. Some certifying groups such as Farm Verified Organic and O.C.I.A., Organic Crop Improvement Association *(see p. 180)*, are interstate groups covering several states, and in the case of FVO, is tied directly to a marketing operation. If a grower is at all interested in organics, he/she would have at least applied to one of these groups. Any products purchased that originated from a certified grower, will have a certificate to back it up. Organic people are proud of the extra time, attention, labor and care they give to their work and are thus very informative about it. They say it on their bags, on the telephone and they send certificates to back it up. If you have to ask a lot of questions, chances are it just isn't organic.

Methods and Definition

Organic farmers enrich their soil with natural fertilizers such as manure, natural rock products, compost, earthworms, beneficial bacteria and algae cultures. Insects are controlled by using predatory insects, insect disease cultures and/or attractants and crop rotation. Weeds are controlled through crop rotation and hand or mechanical cultivation. Rodents are controlled by introduction of rodent predators, traps or natural repellents. Organic does not just stop at the farm, either. Products displaying an organic label are produced, harvested, distributed, stored, processed and packaged without the application of synthetically compounded fertilizers, pesticides, or growth regulators.

Defining Chemical-Free

When there is no written organic certification available, a product which is grown without agricultural chemicals can be listed as "chemical free" under the following circumstances. The state has no organic certification program; the farm is in transition from chemical to natural methods; the product is grown "wild" with neither organics nor chemicals; tests for chemical residues prove none detected. Chemical-Free products are subjected to laboratory analysis which includes testing for different insecticides and pesticides. Those with residue levels in excess of 5% of the level regarded as safe by the Food and Drug Administration are rejected.

We support organic and bio-dynamic farming and believe these methods are necessary for a healthy planet and healthy people. Buy organic whenever possible.

☞ ☞ ☞ *FOOD MAINTAINS LIFE.*
IT IS THE CONDITION OF THAT FOOD THAT WILL DETER-
MINE THE BODY'S ULTIMATE CAPABILITY TO MAINTAIN MAXI-
MUM HEALTH AND NORMAL LONGEVITY. ☜ ☜ ☜

Are Sprouting Seeds Different?

Sprouting seeds are different than standard edible seeds and
beans. Mung beans, for example, can be cooked Indian style or
sprouted Chinese style. Beans for cooking need only be clean of dirt
and chaff. A percentage of those beans, however, will never sprout
and are called hard seed. Hard seed is of no consequence in an
Indian soup or dish because it cooks normally. But to the sprouter,
it is an unpleasant surprise and can even break a tooth!

To eliminate the problem of hard and other unsproutable seed, a
gravity feed system is used to filter out the unsproutables. The
machine detects them because they have a different density and
weight. After a good filtering and cleaning, 100-300 bad seeds may
be removed from a 1,000 seed lot. This, of course, raises the price
of the 700 or so remaining seeds. But the germination ratio of the
remaining seed is guaranteed and is typically in the 96% range.

The percentage of unsproutable seed varies according to farming
techniques, weather and serendipity. Organic farming is, by its very
nature, more labor intensive. Expect to pay more for food grown
this way. But the economics of this kind of farming will improve if
we insist on naturally grown products. Consumers have tremendous
power. In 1990, they literally brought the apple industry to its knees
during the Alar pesticide scare. The result? The apple industry volun-
tarily discontinued Alar usage in advance of the FDA's efforts to regulate it.

Characteristics of Good Sprouting Seed

Organically grown
90+ to 99+ germination
Fast rate of growth
No hard seed
Clean, no debris

Big, unblemished leaves
Shells fall off naturally
Tall and long shoots
One year-plus shelf life
Resistance to root rot

Storage Of Seeds

The Pyramids

Some years ago, an interesting story about seeds was in the news. Wheat berries, it seems, were discovered entombed in one of the great pyramids. Wheat was a treasured grain considered to be the staff of life and was often served up as an offering to the goddess of agriculture by the Greeks and to the Goddess Ceres by the Romans. Even as early as 2,800 B.C. in China, elaborate ceremonies were conducted honoring the cereal grains. But it was the Egyptian goddess Isis who is purported to have discovered the wheat grain in Phoenicia (now Lebanon). The Egyptian kings often buried themselves with wheat so they could have food in the hereafter. *(See Kamut p. 75.)* All this is certainly fascinating, but the real news story here is that after thousands of years, the wheat berries still sprouted.

Don't worry, you are not required to store your sprouting seeds in a pyramid, although modern mini-pyramid domes are available and work well. But there is a lesson of the pyramids: keep your seeds dry, cool and well protected to avoid contamination. In addition to these basic tenets of proper storage, you will need to know a little about the storage characteristics of the different seeds. Armed with this information you can store all your sprouting seeds without fear.

Storing in Jars

Jars are the most common and probably the most successful storage method. First, sterilize the jars, then dry them thoroughly. An oven is a good place to dry your jars because a 200°F. oven sterilizes and dries them at the same time. If you dry your jars outside, bacteria or other micro-organisms, not to mention dust and other particulate matter, may contaminate the jar. Once you have a sterile jar, it is important that you achieve a complete seal. Many lids have rubber washers in them which provide a moisture proof seal. Other jars use cardboard inside the lids, and still others use a silicone coating. All of these methods are better than plain metal to glass which makes an incomplete seal.

Placement is also important. Find a location that is less influenced by the elements--light, temperature and air. Avoid direct sun and heat. Cellars are traditionally the best storage areas. If you store your seeds there, keep your jars elevated so as to avoid mice, vermin and floods. If your quantities are small and manageable in the kitchen, keep them in cabinets. The lower cabinets may be preferable to the higher ones because heat rises and collects in the highest spot.

Plastic Bags, Containers, Cellophane

Plastic 5-6 gallon buckets are excellent for long-term bulk storage as long as the lids contain a rubber gasket or other material to create a perfect seal so that moisture and air are prevented from entering. Plastic bags such as zip-lock bags are fine for small quantities and short periods such as 1-3 months. However, if temperatures are above 75°F., store the bags in the refrigerator or freezer making sure they are tightly sealed and do not contain moisture. Squeeze out excess air before sealing. Cellophane is also suitable for short-term storage. Cellulose is a pulp or paper derivative and is not related to plastic. Many groceries such as cookies, crackers and chips are stored in cellophane or are laminated with polyethylene to provide a stronger bag with a moisture barrier. Cellophane is fine for short term storage, but it has two shortcomings. First, it tears easily and second, it softens in the presence of water. However, pure cellophane is 100% bio-degradable and thus ecologically desirable.

Dry Ice

If cold temperatures are not available through refrigeration or cold cellars, a cold storage environment can be devised using dry ice. When using a plastic storage bucket, place a ½ lb. piece of dry ice on top of 3 inches of grain. Do not let the dry ice contact the bucket as it can deteriorate the plastic! Pour the rest of the grain on top and place the lid on loosely. The ice forms carbon dioxide gas which forces the oxygen out of the bucket. After 12 hours, seal the lid. This procedure provides further protection of your grain from bugs and larva. Dry ice suppliers can be located in your yellow pages.

Bugs

Even with the best packing and storage efforts, your seeds may come with their own pests. Some seeds are contaminated with tiny larvae which are collected with the seeds in the fields. Unfortunately, unless you buy commercial grain which is often sterilized in packaging, naturally grown food often comes with smaller members of the natural community. These tiny larvae are laid on the grain by flying gnats. The gnats may come in with the grain or the grain may already contain larvae when you buy it. Probably the most pesky pest in the USA, and the one that causes the most damage to stored grain, is the Indian meal moth. But don't forget about his friends, the rice weevil, maize weevil, lesser grain borer and the Angoumois grain moth. They live entirely within the kernel, where they feed unseen and usually unsuspected. The larvae hatch into weevils and they in turn change into mealy moths much in the same way a caterpillar turns into a butterfly. They hatch at certain times of the year and in hot weather.

Non-Toxic Solutions

There is no easy solution if your house is already full of bugs. Commercial sprays are not recommended, but if all else fails, obtain the kind used by restaurants which is "officially" approved for use in food establishments. Biological controls, however, are the better way. There are a handful of natural predator insects which do not bother the grain at all. Instead, they eat the pests or parasitize their larvae preventing them from multiplying. True, the natural predators do reproduce but only if they have food. Because they do not eat the grain, they run out of food and die. These "beneficial insects" are harmless to people, animals and the environment.

Another natural solution includes the use of pheromones which is the scent that insects use to communicate with each other. Pheromones have been isolated in the laboratory and essentially perform as an organic sex-attractant. The male insects are attracted to small sticky traps that contain the lure and get stuck. Pheromone traps can work for roaches, flies, beetles and mice as well as moths. *(For more information about pheromone traps see p. 180.)*

Freeze 'em!

If you don't want to be bugged, the best approach is prevention. These bugs have an internal clock which tells them it is summer and thus time to hatch. If you have the space, freeze your seed for 48 hours. The cold kills the larvae and does not hurt the seed. Or, you can keep the bugs guessing by keeping your grains and legumes at 65°F. or less. Heat also kills them. You can spread contaminated foods onto a cookie sheet and bake at 150° F for 2 hours. Heat is okay for foods but not recommended for sprouting seeds because it can sterilize the seed and destroy its germination.

Food grade diatomaceous earth is probably the best preventative measure for large quantities of seed storage. It comes from dried ancient lake beds and is a pure form of silica. Some varieties have been sweetened with milk powder as an attractant. A small amount spread on the walls and inner surfaces of your storage container is all you need. It looks like flour to us, but is like cut glass to an insect. (Glass is composed of silicates). It is harmless to people, animals, birds and the environment, but it kills insects that come in contact with it by causing dehydration. In fact, it is often fed to horses to stop intestinal parasites. Use a paper towel or dry sponge to apply. *Caution:* Do not inhale this fine silica flour/powder. Silica approved face masks are available at hardware stores for your protection.

Grains like rice, wheat, oats, barley and rye are bugged most. Alfalfa is rarely a victim. But sunflowers are the most sensitive of all and should be refrigerated for best results. Sunflowers attract Indian meal moths during the summer season unless you keep them cool. Keep shelled sunflowers refrigerated year-round for best results. They also store well in your freezer. Raw in-the-shell sunflowers can be stored at room temperatures during the Winter. The shell provides protection and extends shelf life. Refrigerate when outside temperatures climb above 70 degrees F.

Sesame seeds and nuts are also vulnerable but are inclined to a different problem. Because of their high fat content, they are subject to rancidity unless refrigerated. Once they have been shelled, the potential for this kind of deterioration is even greater. On the heartier side, legumes like mung, lentil and soy, and vegetable seeds like cabbage, radish, turnip and clover, are rarely affected by bugs and the elements. These seeds will keeps for years with minimal care.

Keep in mind that no matter what seed, if the temperature is cold enough, bugs will never hatch. If you have refrigerator or freezer room, keep the vulnerable seeds refrigerated during the hot summer. But if you cannot, store in a cool, dry spot and try to keep temperatures below 60 degrees. Avoid buying seed in the spring and summer. The best time to purchase seeds is soon after the fall harvest, then store them through the winter. You can stock up in the winter, but in the summertime, it is best not to buy more than you can consume. A little bit of care will go a long way to keeping your whole grains wholesome.

Seeds Sensitivity to Temperature & Storage

HARDY SEEDS	*LESS HARDY*	*VERY DELICATE*
Alfalfa	Barley	Shelled Sunflower
Cabbage	Buckwheat	Whole Sunflower
Red Clover	Corn	
Fenugreek	Peanuts	
Chia	Hard Wheat	
Kale	Soft Wheat	
Mustard	Millet	
Red Radish	Flax	
Turnip	Quinoa	
Psyllium	Oats	
Adzuki	Rye	
Soybean	Triticale	
Green Pea	Lentil	
Mung Bean	Garbanzo	

Column 1 seeds can generally store for multiple years. Column 2 seeds can attract bugs during the summer season and should be kept cool and dry at that time. Column 3 seeds definately require refrigeration during summer and anytime outdoor temperatures climb above 80°F.

Kamut

Egyptian Wheat

If you hear the name *Kamut* get excited. It's wheat. Yes, there are thousands of wheats, all members of the triticum family, but Kamut is different. It's 4,000 years old. It was brought to this country after excavation from an Egyptian tomb near the Nile River in Dahshur, Egypt. Because the tomb was so dry, the grain never lost its vitality. Talk about seed storage! Only 36 kernels were brought to the U.S. in 1950 and planted in Montana. Six years later, 1,500 bushels of this Egyptian borne wheat were produced. Big deal? It wouldn't be, except that this wheat is different. Each kernel is 2½ times larger than common spring wheat and it is 17%-18% protein as compared to an average 12% protein for regular spring wheat. It is also lower in carbohydrates and higher in lipids (fat) so it has more calories. Of course, like all wheat, there is no cholesterol. Kamut is higher in 8 of the 9 minerals commonly found in wheat including significantly more magnesium and zinc. The yield is also better and it is drought-resistant.

No interest was shown in the grain for years and it was sold as cattle feed until the mid-1980's. Today, Kamut (pronounced "ka-moot" after the word for "ancient wheat") is popular in macrobiotic circles and is used in whole wheat pastas and puffed wheat cereals. It sprouts easily and has a delicious wholesome taste--great for sprout breads, cookies and snacks. Although, it is still hard to find, keep your ears open to hear more about this new/old exciting variety of wheat.

Nutritional Value of
Kamut vs. Average Wheat [6]

	AVERAGE WHEAT	KAMUT
WATER	11.5	9.8
PROTEIN	12.3	17.3
FAT	1.9	2.6
CARBOHYDRATE	72.7	68.2
CALCIUM	30.0	31.0
IRON	3.9	4.2
MAGNESIUM	117.0	153.0
PHOSPHORUS	396.0	411.0
POTASSIUM	400.0	446.0
SODIUM	2.0	3.8
ZINC	3.2	4.3
MANGANESE	3.8	3.2
NIACIN	5.31	5.54
THIAMINE	0.42	0.45
RIBOFLAVIN	0.11	0.12

* Water, protein, fat and carbohydrate are percentages of total weight. Minerals and vitamins are in mg per 100 grams weight.

Quinoa

The Ancient Grain

About one hundred and fifty years ago bananas were unknown in the United States and peanuts were only eaten by slaves. So who's to say that an old South American grain called Quinoa (pronounced keen-wa) won't become a popular American staple.

It is uncanny that such a wonderfully tasty and nutritionally important food could be lost, forgotten and even shunned in its native land. Quinoa was grown by the Incas on terraces in the Andes Mountains in Peru, Bolivia and Chile, the same places where it is grown by farmers today. It is a hardy plant which resembles the weed lambs quarters. It thrives in low rainfall, high altitudes and survives when other food crops cannot. The Incas would grind it into flour for breads, biscuits, use its leaves for vegetables, burn the stalks for fuel and use the saponin from its soak water as a soap. But, today, even in areas where production is greatest, it is hard to find quinoa in a restaurant. People are embarrassed to admit knowledge of it because of cultural ignorance and radio and television commercials which promote refined foods imported from other countries. How sad considering they are literally sitting on a nutritional gold mine.

Quinoa contains more protein than any other grain with an average of 16.2% and some varieties as high as 20%. Some wheats come close to matching quinoa's protein content, but corn, barley and rice are no competition. Like soybeans, quinoa is exceptionally high in lysine as well as other amino acids Phenylalanine, Tyrosine, Cystine and Methionine. This makes it very compatible with other grains which, as a group, are low in lysine, and with soybeans which is low in methionine and cystine. In fact, its over all amino acid make-up is similar to milk!

With all its lack of respect, one would think it tastes awful. Nothing could be farther from the truth. Most first-time tasters like it. It cooks quickly (15 minutes) and is light like millet but has a nutty flavor all its own. It is also non-glutinous which means it is not allergy prone and because it is not sticky or heavy, it combines well with cold dishes and is easy to eat in the summertime. Combine quinoa with other flours in bread recipes from corn breads to biscuits. Use it as a holiday stuffing. Mix it in with rice or buckwheat, stuff it into grape leaves, add it to soups, tabooli, salads, tofu casserole and make quinoa pudding in lieu of rice pudding.

As for sprouting, only the agricultural form of the seed will germinate. Quinoa, which is available at health food stores, is for cooking only. A light sheath or skin is removed during processing to make it more palatable. The sheath is bitter. But that is the form in which quinoa sprouts best and it is fast. In just 24 hours, the sprout is practically ¼ inch long! After 2-3 days, a beautiful red and white shoot with a hint of green emerges. It tastes sweet and snack-like. This is sprouted quinoa in its prime. After this, it grows increasingly more bitter and fibrous. Although we do not have nutritional figures for sprouted quinoa, it is safe to say that protein increases, sugar increases and starch decreases.

Selected Mineral Comparison of Grains [8]
Mg per 100 grams of weight

	CALCIUM	PHOSPHORUS	IRON
QUINOA	141.0	449.0	6.6
Wheat	36.0	224.0	4.6
Yellow Corn	6.0	207.0	3.7
White Rice	8.0	143.0	-.-

Quinoa vs. Other Grains [7]
Percent of total content

GRAIN	WATER	PROT	FAT	CARBO	FIBR	ASH*
QUINOA	11.4	16.2	6.9	63.9	3.5	3.3
Barley	11.1	8.2	1.0	78.8	0.5	0.9
Buckwheat	11.0	11.7	2.4	72.9	9.9	2.0
Corn	72.7	3.5	1.0	22.1	0.7	0.7
Millet	11.8	9.9	2.9	72.9	3.2	2.5
Oats	12.5	13.0	5.4	66.1	10.6	3.0
Rice	12.0	7.5	1.9	77.4	.9	1.2
Rye	11.0	9.4	1.0	77.9	0.4	0.7
Wheat	13.0	14.0	2.2	69.1	2.3	1.7

* Water, Protein (represents amino acids), Fats (lipids, oils), Carbohydrates (sugars, starches), Fiber (bran), Ash (minerals).

Latin Names For Sprouting Seeds

Radish	Rahpanus sativus
Wheat	Triticum, T. Vulgare, T. Aestivum
Sunflower	Helianthus, Helianthemum
Fenugreek	Trigonella Fenum Graecum.
Alfalfa	Medicago sativa. Lucerne.
Clover	Trifolium incarnatum
Green Pea	Pisum sativum
Adzuki	Phaseolus Angularis
Mung bean	Phaseolus aureus
Barley	Hordeum spp.
Corn	Zea Mays.
Lentil	Lens culinaris.
Cabbage	Brassica oleracea.
Peanut	Arachis hypogaea.
Quinoa	Quinoa spp.
Buckwheat	Herb. Fagopyrum esculentum or tataricum. (akin to beech tree.)

Jar vs. Vertical sprouter. If you were a sprout, where would you like to grow up? Jars were never designed as gardening tools. They get poor marks for air circulation, water drainage and light.

Red pea sprouts in its 3 stages of growth, at 2 days, 5 days, and 8 days growth. They grow inside the greenhouses in background.

NUTRITION

The great Law of Life is Replenishment. If we do not eat, we die. Just as surely, if we do not eat the kind of food which will nourish the body constructively, we not only die prematurely, but we suffer along the way. - Norman Walker, D.S. at 108 years of age.

Herbal tradition recognizes the medicinal properties of many seeds and plants including their sprouts. In some cases, the medicinal properties of the mature plant are not yet fully realized in the baby plant. In others, the sprouts not only fully embody these medicinal properties but accentuate and intensify them.

Alfalfa

Medico Sativa

Alfalfa, which is known as lucerne in other parts of the world, originated in Armenia and its name in Arabic means "Alf-al-fa," "father of all foods." It is arguably the most widely eaten food on the planet. Animals the world over graze on this plant more than any other and have been doing so since 1,000 years B.C. Still, until very recently, it was virtually overlooked as a food for human consumption.

In ancient times, alfalfa was used mostly as a remedy to build strength and correct illness. Then in 1935, researchers discovered vitamin K, the nutrient which aids blood clotting, and alfalfa began to attract scientific attention. Upon probing more deeply, researchers were amazed by alfalfa's high vitamin and mineral content. Alfalfa, as grown in the field, has a rich concentration of vitamin A, B-complex vitamins, vitamin E, calcium, iron, magnesium, potassium, phosphorus and many important trace minerals. Dehydrated alfalfa grass (as grown in the open field) contains a minimum of 8,000 IU vitamin A (per 100 grams) as compared with 7,500 IU for apricots and 9,000 IU for beef liver. Its protein content can be as much as 40% of the dried grass which is higher than beef or soybeans. It has more than 20,000 IU of vitamin K. Alfalfa is nutrient-rich because its roots reach down to an average depth of 38 feet and have been known to penetrate as far as 66 feet. This enables it to mine out precious mineral resources located in the sub-strata levels of the earth.

These days, folklore remedies are frequently substantiated by modern science and this is definately the case with alfalfa which has an impressive list of therapeutic roles. Among these are cholesterol reduction. Researchers found the fiber in alfalfa pushes cholesterol out of the arteries while its saponins scrub and dissolve it. So impressive was its performance in reducing low density lipoproteins (LDL - the bad kind), that a major research scientist experimented with it on himself. Dr. René Malinow, chief of the cardiovascular disease research center at the Oregon Regional Primate Research has studied alfalfa since the late 1970's and has arguably produced the major body of scientific work on it in modern times. He volunteered himself as a human subject and ate large doses of roasted alfalfa seeds for six week periods over 5 months. His blood cholesterol level dropped 30%. More alfalfa caused an even greater decline, but there were side effects *(see p. 116.)*. Malinow continued his tests on other human subjects and monkeys [40,41,42] and found that alfalfa replaced the LDL's with the more beneficial high density lipoproteins (HDL - the good kind), increasing the HDL by 40%. He also found that steaming the seeds eliminated all potential toxicity [37,42].

Alfalfa tea has been used as a remedy for arthritis, diabetes, rheumatism, ulcers and to promote breast milk in nursing mothers. Doctors in Johannesburg, South Africa were able to lower an 18 year old diabetic's blood sugar levels from 68mg per 100ml to 648mg in 2 hours after drinking alfalfa tea. They attribute the effect to the high levels of manganese in alfalfa [43]. Alfalfa also delivers much estrogenic-like activity through its abundance of plant hormones. In tests with different female animals in different countries, alfalfa proved itself a formidable estrogenic agent [44] which may play a role in the reduction of breast cancer [26]. Historically, alfalfa has been described as a "tonic" because of its rich resources of vitamins, minerals and protein. The relevance of other factors such as isoflavones, flavones and fatty acids is now being explored. The wonders of this ancient miracle food never seem to stop as suggested by an article in *Biosources Digest* (July 1980). They suggested alfalfa be given serious consideration as an alternative energy fuel!

Clover

Trifolium pratense: red clover, incarnatum: crimson clover.

Medicinally, clover is known as a tonic, a nutritive and a blood purifier. Jethro Kloss, the renowned herbalist and author of *Back to Eden*, called it "One of God's greatest blessings to man." Clover is a wonderful source of volatile oils, carbohydrates, amino acids, flavonoids, minerals, vitamins and saponins. Its profuse and exceedingly absorbable calcium and magnesium relaxes the nervous system and settles the stomach. This accounts for its role as a sedative and an anti-spasmodic. A tea made from the blossoms is an expectorant and has been used in the treatment of whooping cough. In the medical books of the nineteenth century, clover was a popular ingredient in body plasters. Its lime, silica and other earthly salts make it an ideal plaster. Plasters were used for sores, boils and cancers. The Shakers used it for cancerous ulcers and burns. Plasters and compresses were also used for childhood skin problems such as eczema and psoriasis. The mineral salts also alkalinize the body and promote detoxification. It had a reputation as a remedy for cancerous growths including cancer of the throat and stomach and was also used for leprosy, pellagra and syphilis.

Red clover flowers are known to promote fertility probably due to its high mineral content. It includes virtually every trace mineral needed by the glands and helps restore and balance hormonal functions. Its estrogenic activity has been linked to its isoflavone content. It may also balance the acid/alkaline environment of the uterus in favor of conception. The sprouts of red clover share many of the medicinal properties of the other leguminosae (alfalfa, pea, soy, lentil) with an emphasis on blood purification, increasing energy and improving weak nerves.

Fenugreek

Trigonella foenum graecum

Fenugreek is actually a member of the legume (leguminosae) family. It is a cousin of clover and lucerne (alfalfa). The Pharaohs of Egypt used it in religious ceremonies. The monks of the Middle Ages grew it to treat blood poisoning, failing eyesight, fevers, palpitations and liver and kidney troubles. It is widely cultivated in Arab countries where it was traditionally used to stimulate appetite. Its chemical composition resembles that of cod-liver oil and is considered a 'sister herb' to garlic, enhancing that herb's disinfectant properties [54]. It is a tonic because it is so rich in many minerals including iron and sulfur and vitamin E. It 'feeds' the blood and is recommended for ailments that are associated with weakness such as anemia and infections. Both the seed and the whole plant are used.

Fenugreek is a demulcent meaning it is soothing to the mucous membranes and reduces inflammations. A tea made from the seed is used as a gargle and for sore throats. It also acts as an expectorant, clearing the mucosa of the chest and respiratory system. Byzantium mothers used it to increase their milk supply. Poultices made from the stalk and leaves have been used on wounds, boils, sores and tumors. The seed contains beneficial volatile oils and steroidal saponins which may be used to regulate blood cholesterol. Fenugreek sprouts have both the properties of the seed as well as the plant. This sprout should be used to stimulate and to fortify.

Nutrition in Fenugreek Seed

(in Milligrams per 100 grams) [30]

Protein	23.0	Zinc	2.50
Calories	323.0	Niacin	1.64
Calcium	176.0	Iron	33.53
Total fat	6.4	Arginine	2.47
Magnesium	191.0	Leucine	1.76
Phosphorus	296.0	Lysine	1.68
Potassium	770.0	Aspartic acid	2.71
Sodium	67.0	Glutamic acid	3.99

Broccoli and Cabbage

Brassica family

The cabbage family of foods includes broccoli, cabbage, Chinese cabbage, kale, turnip, rutabaga, radish, mustard, rape, cauliflower, collard greens, brussel sprouts and kohlrabi. Of these, the first nine are good for home sprouting. This family is rich in fiber and a good source of minerals especially potassium 253mg per 100 grams, sulfur 1710mg and vitamins C 47mg, E and A 200 IU. They have a drying and binding faculty that makes them effective for inflammations and hot swellings. Historically, cabbage was used to combat scurvy at sea even by the famous Captain Cook. Sailors would make sauerkraut from it which coated their intestinal tract with friendly bacteria and promoted regularity. The fermentation from the kraut remedied the complaints of flatulence that are common with the cabbage family. It is also improved by boiling and draining. European literature often mentions cabbage juice as the best medicine for hangovers. Philip Moore in the Hope of Health in 1564 wrote, "the juice of cabbage purges the head, being put into the nostules. Being taken after much drinking, it withstandeth drunkenness."

Broccoli and cabbage and the rest of the brassica family of cruciferous vegetables are now taken seriously at the National Cancer Institute. *(For information on the cancer protecting enzymes in broccoli sprouts, see p. 128.)* Worldwide epidemiological studies consistently point to lower than average cancer rates for those groups regularly eating dark green leafy vegetables. The crucifers contain compounds called glucosinolates which block the development of cancer. Turnip greens contain between 39 and 166 milligrams per hundred grams of glucosinolates. When cooked, the concentration drops to a range of 21-94 [46].

Broccoli and cabbage sprouts have the greatest potential in colon and stomach cancers. Several major epidemiological studies demonstrate that eaters of leafy green crucifers have the lowest colon cancer rates.

Other population surveys add cancers of the prostate, rectum, esophagus, lung and bladder to the list. In May 1978, Lee Wattenberg, M.D., a professor of pathology at the University of Minnesota Medical school, reported in the journal Cancer Research, that he had isolated chemicals called indoles from cruciferous vegetables which were potent antidotes to development of cancer. Without the indoles, 91% of his rats developed tumors. With the indoles, only 21% succumbed. Subsequently, other important anti-cancer and detoxification compounds were found in cabbage. Dithiolthiones in cabbage cause the body to release glutathiones, a natural body enzyme. Glutathiones neutralize or detoxify carcinogens before they damage the DNA. The greater the supply of glutathione, the greater the protection against cancer. Another anti-cancer compound, sulphoraphane, stimulates the cell's production of quinone reductase, an enzyme that blocks tumor growth. *(See p. 121.)*

Cancer starts because DNA, the cellular genetic material, is damaged by a carcinogen. This could be a pollutant from air or water, cigarette smoke, pesticides, ionizing radiation, free radicals, etc. The mutated cells then start to divide abnormally. Consistent, low level doses of anti-cancer enzymes found in foods like cabbage, enhance the body's biological barriers to the cancer development. These enzymes are proving to be our natural artillery in the cellular battle to protect the good cells from going cancerous in the presence of carcinogens. The consumption of sprouts from the cabbage family is the best source of these enzymes because enzymes abound during the rapid growth period of germination.

Radish
Raphanus sativus, cruciferae

Radish belongs to the crucifer family and is thus a cousin of cabbage, turnip and mustard. Many of the medicinal properties of the crucifers apply to radish as well. The ribbons of red in the colorful leaves of this sprout properly telegraph the palatery inferno awaiting the unwary gourmet. Radish sprouts actually produce more BTU's of heat than the mature radish bulb. The sprouts are definitely expectorants. They clear mucous from the respiratory tract and thus are wonderful for such ailments as colds, sinus congestion, bronchitis, whooping cough and for the long term improvement of asthma. Seeds can be used in plasters like mustard. Poultices made from the seeds or ground up sprouts may be placed over various parts of the body with benefit. They relieve chest congestion when placed on the chest in a plaster, poultice or salve and help rheumatism when placed over the shoulders, wrists and knees. Foot baths made from ground seeds or blended sprouts relieve head congestion.

Radish is wonderful for the entire intestinal tract from the nose to the anus. Its heat producing action stimulates the elimination of excess mucous and thus starts a cleansing process which can include expelling worms. (Intestinal flora like it.) It is anti-putrefactive and antiseptic. Too much radish, however, will induce vomiting (emetic). Small amounts, on the other hand, stimulate appetite. Sprouted radish is excellent nourishment during cold weather. It is an effective diuretic and restorative for troubles of the urinary tract, bladder and kidneys.

Mustard

Brassica nigra

Sprouters prefer black mustard because yellow mustard is a gelatinous seed and harder to germinate. In herbal tradition, mustard was used as a plaster, a stimulant and an emetic (encourage vomiting). Put into a foot bath, the ground seeds will draw the blood from the head and lungs thus relieving headache and congestion. Its main use is as an external stimulant. Its rubefacient action causes mild irritation to the skin, but stimulates the circulation and relieves muscular pain. For chest congestion and bronchitis, blend mustard seeds or sprouts into a poultice and place on chest. A drink of the blended sprouts or seeds stimulates perspiration (diaphoretic) which is ideal for reducing fevers and remedying colds and flu. To induce vomiting, simply drink copious amounts of tea made from steeping the seeds in hot water. To make plasters, mix 1 part of mustard meal with 4 parts of flour.

Sunflower

Helianthus annus

The sunflower is 3,000 years old and is so named because its golden rayed flowers are reminiscent of the sun. It is heliotropic, meaning it follows and faces the sun from morning to night. Extensive root systems extract many trace minerals not always present in top soil. The seed is the primary medicinal part. It is rich in the following nutrients: phosphorous and calcium, excellent for bones and teeth, fat and carbohydrate digestion, muscle and tissue tone and the nervous system; Iron, for healthy red blood corpuscles; Copper, necessary in minute quantities for the utilization of iron; Iodine, mostly found in sea vegetables; Potassium, predominant in brain tissue and necessary for proper functioning of the nervous system; Magnesium, for muscle tissue brain and lungs. The seed contains as much as 30% protein and is a good source of niacin, the skin vitamin. It contains 92 USP units of Vitamin D, rarely found in vegetables. Historically, herbalists made a syrup of the sunflower leaves for the treatment of malaria, pulmonary problems, sore throat, coughs, bronchitis and disease of the kidneys. In Russian folk medicine, they make a liniment from the sunflower head using vodka and apply it externally for rheumatic pain. The stem parts were used in tea for fevers. North American Indians made an extract from the roots for snake bite and used the oil from the seed as a hair tonic. The seeds are extremely nourishing and enhance endurance.

Nutrition of Organic Sunflower Seeds
(in Milligrams per 100 grams) [30]

Iron	6.77	Vitamin A	50.00IU
Vitamin E	52.18	Vitamin D	92.0USP
Calcium	116.00	Total lipids	49.57
Phosphorus	705.0	Linoleic Acid	30.00
Zinc	5.06	Niacin	4.50
Copper	1.75	Riboflavin	0.25
Sulfur	87.0	Thiamin	2.29
Magnesium	354.0	Glutamic acid	5.58
Protein	22.78	Aspartic acid	2.45
Potassium	689.00	Arginine	2.40
Leucine	1.66		

Green Peas
Pisum Sativum

Even a common food like green pea has medicinal benefits. The population of Tibet has remained stationary for about 200 years because of their diet, which is rich in barley and green peas. Upon investigation, the anti-fertility compound m-xylohydro-quinone was isolated [48]. Although, we are not recommending peas as an oral contraceptive, those who are having difficulty conceiving should consider reducing their consumption of peas and pea sprouts.

Because peas are legumes, they are rich in protease inhibitors that prevent certain viruses and chemicals that promote cancer. As rich sources of fiber, they are useful in reducing the LDL (bad) cholesterol in the blood. They also help control blood sugar thus making them a good food for diabetics. Peas have also been linked to a reduction in the occurrence of appendicitis and, in a study on dogs, temporarily decreased their blood pressure [46].

Lentil, Mung, Adzuki, China Red Pea, Chick Pea
Lens culinaris, Phaseolus aureus + angularis, Cicer Arietinum

Beans have always been said to be "good for the heart." Now we know why. They clear out the dangerous LDL cholesterol in the blood. Simply by eating beans, one man brought down his cholesterol from 274 to 190; another lowered it from 218 to 167. The reason? Primarily their soluble fiber. Fiber lowers blood pressure among vegetarians and bean eaters [49]. Sprouting increases bean fiber by 300%.

Beans are also marvelous regulators of insulin. They make very gradual changes in blood sugar and do not draw on the body's natural insulin to keep blood sugar under control. In fact, they provide more receptors for insulin to land, controlling the loss of insulin back into the bloodstream.

Beans contain at least two powerful cancer blocking substances, lignans and protease inhibitors. Lignans fight breast and colon cancer after being turned into hormone-like substances by bacteria in the colon. Protease inhibitors actually turn off the oncogenes--genetic material in every cell that when activated commences the process of mutagenic cell division. Protease inhibitors are strictly preventative. They prevent normal cells from going cancerous. Sprouting dramatically increases this enzyme activity [46].

Beans contain complex sugars that are attacked by bacteria in the large intestine and release gas. These sugars are easily removed by rinsing repeatedly as in sprouting and/or boiling and discarding the water. Studies show that legume eaters become physiologically accustomed to the sugars with the continuity of regular bean meals.

Soybean
Glycine Max
The soybean is truly a revolutionary food and is as much a staple in Asia as dairy and potatoes are in the USA. As with other legumes, research on soybeans confirms its capacity to lower cholesterol in humans and to protect against cancer through its healthy amount of protease inhibitors [50]. It is a wonderful food for the prevention of strokes, high blood pressure, heart disease and atherosclerosis. One woman on a soybean diet not only reduced her cholesterol from 332 to 206 milligrams per deciliter and her triglycerides from 68 to 59, but also reversed the progression of her arterial heart disease by increasing the blood flow to her heart [46].

Soybeans also keep the blood sugar under control. It is number 2 (after peanuts) on the "glycemic index," a list compiled by Dr. David Jenkins charting foods with the least propensity to raise blood sugar. In an experiment with animals eating milk protein (casein) vs. soy protein, 58% of the milk eating animals developed gall stones while only 14% of the soy eaters succumbed. Afterwards, the milk eaters switched to soy and actually reversed and reduced their gallstones! [46]

Soybeans are rich sources of natural plant estrogens which could assist in contraception. Although high estrogen levels have been linked to increasing the risk of breast cancer, estrogen from legumes may help desensitize breast tissue to the excess human estrogen. In one study, a soybean diet reduced the incidence of breast tumors in rats.

Garlic
Allium sativum

The reputation of garlic and onion for therapeutic use is widespread and well respected even amongst the scientific orthodoxy. Garlic's value for treating the common cold is due to the expectorant action of allicin which is also the compound responsible for the famous odor. The volatile oils irritate the stomach which signals the lungs to release mucous in order to expel it. By keeping mucous moving through the lungs, garlic aids in the prevention and treatment of bronchitis, whooping cough, colds, flu and other respiratory ailments. Historically, garlic poultices were placed on the chest to relieve congestion.

Garlic's reputation as an antibiotic is pervasive. The medical literature contains approximately 125 scientific papers on the herb in the last 5 years. Tests even found raw garlic more powerful than penicillin and tetracycline! Garlic is antiseptic, anti-viral, anti-fungal, anti-parasitic, anti-protozoan, anti-spasmodic, anti-microbial and diaphoretic (produces perspiration). It has the broadest spectrum of any anti-microbial agent known. It was used as an anti-infective and anti-parasitic as early as 1500's. It actually chases pathogens out of the intestine while providing a positive environment for friendly bacteria [53]. Even the Egyptians, in a medical paper from 1500 B.C. listed garlic as a prescription for twenty-two complaints among them gastrointestinal disorders, snake-bites, rheumatism, hemorrhoids, ulcers, headache and others. Hippocrates also prescribed garlic. Louis Pasteur confirmed it killed bacteria and Dr. Albert Schweitzer used it against typhus and cholera. In fact, garlic was the drug of choice against tuberculosis and dysentery during World War I [46].

Garlic's reputation crosses cultural and international barriers. Europeans have used it for centuries. In the Soviet Union, it is known as "Russian Penicillin." The Japanese use Kyolic, an odorless cold-processed raw garlic, as an antibiotic. Even the Chinese, with their extensive repertoire of herbal medicines, have used it successfully to combat the frequently fatal disease meningitis. They concluded that part of the cure had to do with garlic's capacity to stimulate the immune system. Dr. Tarig Abdullah and his colleagues at the Akbar Clinic and Research Center in Panama City, Florida would agree. They tested 27 individuals and fed part of the group 12-15 cloves per day. Even the investigators ate the garlic! The blood from the garlic eating group destroyed 140 to 160 percent more cancer cells than the blood from the non-garlic eaters. Garlic is a powerful anti-oxidant. Fresh garlic completely wiped out breast cancers in mice. In a population study in China, residents of Shandongate ate about seven cloves of garlic per day while their neighbors in Quixia rarely had any. The rate of gastric cancer deaths per 100,000 persons in the first town was 3.45 vs. 40 in the second. The national Cancer Institute puts sulfur compounds from garlic and onion high on its list of natural "chemo-preventives." [46]

Evidence is strong that garlic can lower cholesterol, triglycerides, LDL's and blood pressure in both laboratory and clinical studies [52]. The studies on cholesterol along with work on lowering blood pressure and blood sugar have reinforced garlic's reputation as a powerful blood purifier. The Indian researcher Arun K. Bordia found that a diet heavy in garlic prevented the formation of dangerous blood clots even in patients with coronary heart disease. Dr. Eric Block, head of the department of chemistry at the State University of New York at Albany, found that a chemical in garlic is as potent a blood-clot inhibitor as the most famous blood thinning drugs: aspirin. (Blood clots cause heart attacks and strokes.) Indian Dr. M. Sucur fed 5 cloves of fresh garlic to 200 patients daily with extra high blood cholesterol. Virtually all lowered their cholesterol and it took only 2 cloves per day to keep it low [46].

Unfortunately, we don't eat enough garlic. The revulsion to its overpowering odor has the effect of reducing consumption to a level too low to achieve its primary medical benefits. Fortunately, sprouted garlic and onion chives, reduce the famous odor due to the presence of live chlorophyll, an odor neutralizer. Many commercial products claiming odor-free benefits may not be effective because they remove or alter allicin, the primary therapeutic component. Therefore, the sprouted chives, taken in a daily salad, may be the most palatable way to acquire this herb's magical medicine.

The Miracle of Germination

Seeds are a storehouse of vitamins, minerals, enzymes and essential fatty acids as well as the greatest source of protein in the vegetable kingdom. When sprouting, a seed unfolds and starts to multiply and develop its nutrients in order to provide nourishment for the maturing vegetable. This miracle of nature means that a little sunflower seed has in it the basic formula for nourishing a six foot plant.

Germination initiates the following changes in the seed:

1) Nutrients are broken down and simplified: protein into amino acids, fats into essential fatty acids, starches to sugars and minerals chelate or combine with protein in a way that increases their utilization. These processes all increase nutrition and improve digestion and assimilation. This is the reason sprouts are considered predigested food [2].

2) Proteins, vitamins, enzymes, minerals and trace minerals multiply from 300 to 1200 per cent.

3) Chlorophyll develops in green plants.

4) Certain acids and toxins which ordinarily would interfere with digestion are reduced and/or eliminated.

5) Size and water content increase dramatically.

Protein

These miniature green vegetables are high in protein when compared to common green leafy vegetables such as spinach and lettuce, but have less protein than bean sprouts such as soybean, lentil, and chickpea. Alfalfa and sunflower are richer in protein than spinach or any of the common lettuces and they are free of agricultural pesticides and poisons. Alfalfa seed can be as high as 39.8% protein although it reduces its concentration as it grows [3]. On the other hand, lettuce and spinach only supply the nutrients developed from one seed, whereas a sprout salad serves up the nutrition from thousands of seeds.

Protein Content of Sprouts
and Other Vegetarian Foods

Grams per 100 grams edible portion of fresh sprouts [30]

39.8	Alfalfa dry grass	6.2	Navy Bean Sprouts
36.5	Soybeans dry bean	6.2	Garlic
26.6	Wheat germ	4.0	Alfalfa Sprouts
26.0	Peanuts	3.8	Radish Sprouts
24.7	Lentils dry bean	3.6	Broccoli
24.2	Mung dry bean	3.6	Parsley
24.0	Sunflower seed	3.5	Sweet Corn
23.0	Fenugreek seed	3.2	Spinach
18.6	Almonds	3.1	Mung Sprouts
16.6	Chia seed	2.7	Mushrooms
13.1	Soybean sprouts	2.1	Potatoes with skin
13.3	Buckwheat	1.6	Romaine Lettuce
12.6	Hard Winter Wheat	1.3	Avocado
9.0	Lentil Sprouts	1.3	Cabbage
8.8	Green Pea Sprouts	1.3	Looseleaf Lettuce
7.5	Brown Rice	1.1	Banana
6.3	Fresh Green Peas	0.2	Apple

Alfalfa dry grass is Indian ranger variety (Medicago Sativa) field grass dehydrated [3]. Other values are fresh foods and sprouts except where 'dry' is indicated.

Protein Comparison Of Lettuce & Sprouts

Protein in grams per 100 gram amount. [30]

Common Lettuce		*Sprouts*	
0.9	Iceberg	4.0	Alfalfa Sprouts
1.3	Cos, Looseleaf	4.0	Sunflower Sprouts
1.6	Romaine Lettuce	3.8	Radish Sprouts
1.7	New Zeal Spinach	3.1	Mung Sprouts

All values are for fresh produce and sprouts.

The sprouting seeds builds new protein from stored starches, sugars and fats within the seed. Tests prove that all amino acids increase during germination peaking generally between the 5th and 9th days depending on the variety [31]. In fact, the total dry weight protein of legume sprouts such as mung compares favorably to legendary protein foods like eggs and meat. Legumes fall short only in the amino acid methionine [32]. Here protein complementation with another food or sprout rich in sulfur amino acids would achieve a balanced protein. Jeffrey Bland, PhD and Barbara Berquist, authors of a 1980 chemical analysis of alfalfa, lentil and mung sprouts, made this comment about protein.

> *The germinating seed represents a protein manufacturing machine which is turning out protein free of charge on the kitchen sink along with the necessary vitamins and minerals for its assimilation and utilization* [4].

Amino Acid Content of Wheat & Oat Sprouts
On the 5th, 7th and 9th day of germination
In Milligrams per 100 gram portion of sprouts [4].

AMINO ACID	SPROUTED WHEAT			SPROUTED OATS		
	5TH	7TH	9TH	5TH	7TH	9TH
ARGININE	1.8	.9	.9	.9	.9	1.8
ASPARTIC ACID	1.5	2.0	3.0	2.0	.5	1.0
GLUTAMIC ACID	.8	.6	.5	.4	.5	1.6
LEUCINE	.1	.1	.25	.1	.2	.1
LYSINE	0.0	0.0	2.0	0.0	0.0	0.0
METHIONINE	.3	.35	.2	.2	.3	.2
THREONINE	.2	.4	.2	.45	.3	1.0
TYROSINE	0	.1	.15	.2	.01	.1
VALINE	0.07	.07	.06	.07	.07	.07

Values are for fresh sprouts

Protein Comparison of
Dried Sprouts vs. Common Foods
In Milligrams per 100 gram portion of sprouts [4]

	Sprout Soy	Sprout Sunflwr	Sprout Lentil	Sprout Mung	Meat	Egg
TRYPTOPHAN	.159	.06	.216	0.180	.220	0.211
THREONINE	.503	.15	.896	0.765	.830	.637
ISOLEUCINE	.580	.21	1.316	1.351	.984	.850
LYSINE	.752	.12	1.528	1.667	1.642	.819
METHIONINE	.138	.07	.180	.265	.466	.401
PHENYLALANINE	.641	.20	1.104	1.167	.733	.739
VALINE	.620	.21	1.30	1.440	1.044	.950
TOTAL PROTEIN	28%	4%	25%	24%	19%	13%

Values represent fresh product for soy sprout, meat and egg and dry sunflower, lentil and mung sprouts.

Minerals

Next to sea vegetables, sprouts are the best source of minerals and trace minerals. Most salad sprouts are rich in calcium and magnesium, have more phosphorus than fish, and are excellent sources of hard to find trace minerals such as tritium, selenium, manganese, chromium and others. Because minerals and trace minerals are naturally chelated in the sprout, they are more easily utilized by our bodies. Zinc in alfalfa sprouts increases from 6.8mg in the seed (per 100gms), to 18 mg in the sprout (dried weight). One cup (100mg) of alfalfa sprouts provides twice the U.S. RDA of zinc [4].

Mineral Comparison of Alfalfa Seed, Alfalfa Sprouts, and Common Lettuce

Per 100 grams dry weight [3]

	CALC	MAGN	SOD	POT	IRON
ALFALFA SEED	140.00	3.60	.15	980.	10.0
ALFALFA SPROUT	210.00	440.00	29.00	870.	12.0
ICEBERG	20.00	11.00	9.00	175.	.5
COS, LOOSELEAF	68.00	--.	9.00	264.	1.4
BOSTON, BIBB	35.00	--.	9.00	264.	2.0
SPINACH	93.00	88.00	71.00	470.	3.1
NEW ZEAL SPINACH	58.00	40.00	159.00	795.	2.6
ENDIVE	81.00	10.00	14.00	294.	1.7

Values represent dry weight content, not fresh sprouts. Left column includes iceberg lettuce, cos or looseleaf lettuce, Boston or bibb lettuce, New Zealand spinach. Values on top columns are for Calcium, Magnesium, Sodium, Potassium and Iron.

Trace Mineral Content of Sprouts and Seeds

Milligrams per 100 grams dry weight [4]

	MUNG LIGHT	MUNG DARK	ALFAL LIGHT	ALFAL DARK	LENTIL LIGHT	LENTIL DARK	LENTIL SEED	ALFAL SEED	MUNG SEED
CA	100.	79.	200.	210.	74.	59.	62.	140.	120.
MG	310.	310.	410.	440.	190.	160.	180.	360.	290.
NA	7.3	6.	25.	29.	25.	7.8	3.4	0.15	2.1
K	1100.	990.	890.	870.	820.	750.	800.	980.	1200.
FE	7.	6.2	11.	12.	10.	8.9	10.	10.	5.8
SI	54.	55.	46.	41.	50.	55.	27.	51.	51.
MN	1.4	1.6	2.1	2.4	1.9	1.8	1.7	1.8	1.5
ZN	5.4	4.3	17.	19.	6.3	5.4	4.3	6.8	3.1
CR	0.24	0.23	0.21	0.26	0.26	0.18	0.14	0.21	0.21
SE	0.14	0.12	0.13	0.14	0.12	0.12	0.12	0.15	0.12
V	0.04	0.08	0.008	0.008	0.076	0.05	0.008	0.008	0.03

Values represent dry weight content, not fresh sprouts. CA calcium, FE iron, K potassium, MN manganese, MG magnesium, NA sodium, SE selenium, SI silicon, V vanadium, ZN zinc, ALFAL=alfalfa.

Mineral Content of Fresh Sprouted Beans Vs. Other Vegetarian Foods

Milligrams per 100 grams edible portion [30A]

	CALC	IRON	MAG	PHOS	POT
ALFALFA	32.0	0.96	27	70	79
RADISH	51.0	0.86	44	113	86
MUNG	13	0.91	21	54	149
LENTIL	25	3.1	37	173	322
GREEN PEA	36	2.26	65	165	381
SOYBEAN	67	2.10	72	164	484
NAVY PEA	15	1.93	101	100	307
POTATOES	5	0.35	25	50	391
SPINACH	58	0.80	39	28	130
MILK	119	.05	13	93	152
EGGS	56	2.09	12	180	130
LETTUCE	36	1.10	6	45	290

Values represent fresh sprouted beans with 70%-95% water content. Milk whole 3.5% fat. New Zealand spinach. Calc-calcium, Mag-magnesium, Phos-phosphorus, Pot-potassium.

Chlorophyll is often awarded top position as the primary nutritional factor in green leafy sprouts. All green plants transform sunlight into food through photosynthesis. This is a miraculous natural event. Imagine--manufacturing nutrients from sunlight, oxygen and water! Although human beings do not have this wondrous skill, we do manufacture one nutrient from sunlight. We form vitamin D on our skin through the interaction of sunlight, cholesterol and calcium. In fact, it is estimated that we make all the vitamin D we need from just a few minutes exposure to sunshine each day. Green plants and grasses are the richest sources of chlorophyll grown on land. Chlorophyll improves the functioning of the heart and cleanses the vascular system, lungs, liver, and colon. Used as an effective treatment for anemia, it nourishes, purifies and rejuvenates the bloodstream.

Vitamins

Baby green sprouts, like all green vegetables, are an excellent source of B-vitamins. B-vitamins like riboflavin, thiamin, folic acid, biotin, lecithin (choline and inositol) and others increase an average of 4 to 16 times during the first 7 days of germination. Some factors increase even more. B-12, the elusive vitamin alleged to be unavailable to vegetarians, increases almost 2000%, Vitamin B-17, also known as laetrile, multiplies 50 to 100 times that of the original seed. Nucleic acids, fundamental agents of cell growth and regeneration, increase up to thirty times upon sprouting [3].

Mung and lentil beans have almost no vitamin C but their sprouts have a considerable amount. Mung bean sprouts are not only rich in vitamin C, but a good source of the amino acid methionine which is lacking in other sprouts. The light and dark study *(see p. 98.)* verifies that cellular building is enhanced in the presence of light. Vitamin C synthesis increased approximately 25% in the light and protein increased 12%. Even trace mineral levels were higher in the light than those in the dark. No detectable levels of toxic metals such as lead, cadmium, arsenic and mercury were found.

Vitamin Content of Sprouts and Other Vegetarian Foods

Milligrams per 100 grams edible portion [30A].

	ASCORB	THIAM	RIBOFL	NIACIN
ALFALFA	8.2	0.076	0.126	0.481
RADISH	28.9	0.102	0.103	2.853
MUNG BEAN	13.2	0.084	0.124	0.749
LENTIL	16.5	0.228	0.128	1.128
GREEN PEA	10.4	0.225	0.155	3.088
SOYBEAN	15.3	0.340	0.118	1.148
RAW SPINACH	28.1	0.078	0.189	0.724

	PANTO	B6	FOLA	VIT A
ALFALFA	0.563	0.034	36.0	155.0
RADISH	0.733	0.285	94.7	391.0
MUNG BEAN	0.380	0.088	60.8	21.0
LENTIL	0.578	0.190	9.9	45.0
GREEN PEA	1.029	0.265	144.0	166.0
SOYBEAN	0.929	0.176	171.8	11.0
RAW SPINACH	0.065	0.065	194.4	6715.0

Values are for fresh sprouts. Listed in milligrams (mg) except for Folacin in micrograms (mcg) and Vitamin A in International units (IU). Ascorbic acid (vitamin C), Thiamin (vitamin B1), Riboflavin (vitamin B2), Niacin, Pantothenic acid and Vitamin B6.

Selected Nutrient Comparison of
Alfalfa & Radish Sprouts
vs. Whole Milk & Raw Egg
Milligrams per 100 grams edible portion [30A].

	MEASURE	ALFALFA	RADISH	MILK	EGG
Water	g	91.14	90.07	87.99	74.57
Calories	kcal	29.	41	61.	158.
Protein	g	3.99	3.81	3.29	12.14
Fat	g	0.69	2.53	3.34	11.15
Carbohydrate	g	3.78	3.06	4.66	1.20
Fiber	g	1.64	0.53	0.0	0.0
MINERALS					
Calcium	mg	32.	51.	119.	56.
Iron	mg	0.96	0.86	0.05	2.09
Magnesium	mg	27.	44	13.	12.
Phosphorus	mg	70.	113.	93.	180.
Potassium	mg	79.	86.	152.	130.
Sodium	mg	6.	6.	49.	138.
Zinc	mg	0.92	0.56	0.38	1.44
Copper	mg	0.157	0.120	-.-	-.-
Manganese	mg	0.188	0.260	-.-	-.-
VITAMINS					
Ascorbic Acid	mg	8.2	28.9	.94	0.0
Thiamin	mg	0.076	0.102	0.038	0.087
Riboflavin	mg	0.126	0.103	0.162	0.301
Niacin	mg	0.481	2.853	0.084	0.062
Pantothenic	mg	0.563	0.733	0.314	1.727
Vitamin B6	mg	0.034	0.285	0.042	0.120
Folacin	mcg	36.0	94.7	5.0	65.0
Vitamin A	IU	155.0	391.0	126.0	520.0

Values are for fresh sprouts, whole milk with 3.3% fat and raw egg. Calories measured in kilocalories.

Selected Nutrient Comparison of Lentil, Mung & Green Pea Sprouts vs. Whole Milk & Baked Potato

Milligrams per 100 grams edible portion [30A].

	Measure	Pea	Lentil	Mung	Milk	Potato
Water	g	62.27	67.34	90.40	87.99	75.42
Food energy	kcal	128.0	106.0	30.0	61.0	93.0
Protein	g	8.80	8.96	3.04	3.29	1.96
Total fat	g	0.68	0.55	0.18	3.34	0.10
Carbohydrate	g	28.26	22.14	5.93	4.66	21.56
Fiber	g	2.78	3.05	0.81	0.	0.38
Ash	g	1.14	1.00	0.44	0.72	0.97
MINERALS						
Calcium	mg	36.0	25.0	13.0	119.0	5.0
Iron	mg	2.26	3.21	0.91	0.05	0.36
Magnesium	mg	56.0	37.0	21.0	13.0	25.0
Phosphorus	mg	165.0	173.0	54.0	93.0	50.0
Potassium	mg	381.0	322.0	149.0	152.0	391.0
Sodium	mg	20.0	11.0	6.0	49.0	5.0
Zinc	mg	1.05	1.51	0.41	0.38	0.29
Copper	mg	0.272	0.352	0.164	-.	0.215
Manganese	mg	0.438	0.506	0.188	-.	0.161
VITAMINS						
Ascorbic Acid	mg	10.40	16.50	13.20	0.94	12.80
Thiamin	mg	0.225	0.228	0.084	0.038	0.105
Riboflavin	mg	0.155	0.128	0.124	0.162	0.021
Niacin	mg	3.088	1.128	0.749	0.084	1.395
Pantothenic	mg	1.029	0.578	0.380	0.314	0.555
Vitamin B6	mg	0.265	0.190	0.088	0.042	0.301
Folacin	mcg	144.0	99.9	60.8	5.0	9.1
Vitamin A	IU	166.0	45.0	21.0	126.0	-.-

Fresh sprouts green pea, mung and lentil, compared with equal portions of whole milk 3.3% fat and baked potato (without skin).

Sprouts Are More Than Nutrients!

Nutrients are not everything. The German philosopher Goethe said "the whole is more than the sum of its parts." Modern medicine could learn a lot from his observation.

Research is typically directed to locating, defining and demonstrating the effect of chemical substances. But Western science is reluctant to accept the existence of a "life force". Today's doctors are curious about the marvels of ancient Chinese medicine, but only to the point of acupuncture as anesthesia or the pharmacology of its herbs. But Qi (pronounced chi), the vital energy which is the basis of all Chinese medicine is an objectionable idea to western science. Science explains energy in terms of calories. But calories cannot explain life and it is precisely this vital "Qi" energy which controls our health and our ability to recover from illness and injury.

Spectral chromatography is a means of photographing substances and analyzing its nutrition according to its light, color and structure. A chromographic study was made of sprouted wheat in which a snapshot of its growth was taken each day. A ring of life or halo appeared after the first day and continued to intensify each day. Numerous enzymatic processes were visible, starch was breaking up, pink hues of pure thiamin were abundant as were the spokes of protein. Under ultra-violet light, fluorescent rings indicated the presence of niacin and riboflavin. The overall intensity of the color and form gave it a sign of life. The same wheat was broken apart into its germ, bran and kernel and its analysis demonstrated no signs of life in the separate parts. No part reflected a living entity, neither kernel nor germ. A third test was made of the same wheat after it was cooked at 212°F. It would not germinate at all and on the second day, it fell apart. The proteins faded and although enzymes were present in the chromograph, they were employed in the process of decay not growth [11].

The difference between growth and decay is essentially the difference between life and death. Sprout eaters have always known they were getting live nourishment. This life energy or Qi is a lot more than just the sum of the seed's nutritional parts. Dead seed or food with low viability does not deliver the "halo" of life. The old adage: *You are what you eat* holds true. Living foods should be a part of everyone's daily diet, else we must ask the question: Do we eat to live or live to eat?

> *How strange a creature is man, who will at times*
> *go to such extremes to preserve his life, only to shorten*
> *it at the dinner table.* - William H. Gordon.

Energy Content of Sprouts
& Other Vegetarian Foods
Calories per 100 grams edible portion [30A]

128	Green Pea Sprouts	32	Broccoli
122	Soybean Sprouts	30	Mung Sprouts
106	Lentil Sprouts	29	Alfalfa Sprouts
93	Baked Potato	18	Looseleaf Lettuce
67	Navy Bean Sprouts	17	Celery
62	Pinto Bean Sprouts	14	N. Zealand Spinach
42	Carrots	14	Bibb Lettuce
41	Radish Sprouts		

Values for sprouts are for live, fresh sprouts.

"Exclusive concern with individual nutrients is not only unscientific but also potentially dangerous," says Dr. Walter Mertz. Each food is a vast chemical factory of perhaps 10,000 or more elements. Scientists, who once saw foods as mere collections of individual nutrients, are now vigorously beginning to explore their larger pharmacological complexities. For example, "We know how much zinc is in human milk on which a baby grows beautifully. Now we put that same amount of zinc in an infant formula and we find that the infant will not grow. It is identical...as close to human milk as possible, but the zinc won't do it. There is something else in human milk that renders zinc more effective. We don't know what it is." [46]

Nutrient Content of Alfalfa & Radish Sprouts
vs. Iceberg Lettuce & New Zealand Spinach
Milligrams per 100 grams fresh produce [30A]

	MEASURE	ALFALFA	RADISH	LETTUCE	SPINACH
Water	g	91.14	90.07	95.89	94.0
Calories	kcal	29.	41	13.	14.
Protein	g	3.99	3.81	1.01	1.50
Fat	g	0.69	2.53	0.19	0.20
Carbohydrate	g	3.78	3.06	2.09	2.50
Fiber	g	1.64	0.53	-.-	0.70
MINERALS					
Calcium	mg	32.	51.	19.	58.
Iron	mg	0.96	0.86	0.50	0.80
Magnesium	mg	27.	44	9.	39.
Phosphorus	mg	70.	113.	20.	28.
Potassium	mg	79.	86.	158.	130.
Sodium	mg	6.	6.	9.	130.
Zinc	mg	0.92	0.56	0.22	-.-
Copper	mg	0.157	0.120	0.028	-.-
Manganese	mg	0.188	0.260	0.151	-.-
VITAMINS					
Ascorbic Acid	mg	8.2	28.9	3.9	30.0
Thiamin	mg	0.076	0.102	0.046	0.040
Riboflavin	mg	0.126	0.103	0.030	0.130
Niacin	mg	0.481	2.853	0.187	0.500
Pantothenic	mg	0.563	0.733	0.046	0.312
Vitamin B6	mg	0.034	0.285	0.040	-.-
Folacin	mcg	36.0	94.7	56.0	-.-
Vitamin A	IU	155.0	391.0	330.0	4400.0
AMINO ACIDS					
Threonine	g	0.134	-.-	0.053	-.-
Isoleucine	g	0.143	-.-	0.075	-.-
Leucine	g	0.267	-.-	0.070	-.-
Lysine	g	0.214	-.-	0.075	-.-
Valine	g	0.145	-.-	0.062	-.-

Radish Sprouts vs. Mature Radish Vegetable
Milligrams per 100 grams edible portion [30A]

	MEASURE	RADISH SPROUT	MATURE RADISH
Water	g	90.07	95.37
Calories	kcal	41.	14.0
Protein	g	3.81	1.10
Fat	g	2.53	0.10
Carbohydrates	g	3.06	2.63
Fiber	g		0.70
Ash	g	0.53	0.80
MINERALS			
Calcium	mg	51.	27.0
Iron	mg	0.86	0.80
Magnesium	mg	44.	9.0
Phosphorus	mg	113.	28.0
Potassium	mg	86.	280.0
Sodium	mg	6.	16.0
Zinc	mg	0.56	
Copper	mg	0.120	
Manganese	mg	0.260	
VITAMINS			
Ascorbic Acid	mg	28.900	29.00
Thiamin	mg	0.102	0.030
Riboflavin	mg	0.103	0.020
Niacin	mg	2.853	0.300
Pantothenic acid	mg	0.733	0.184
Vitamin B6	mg	0.285	0.075
Folacin	mcg	94.7	14.0
Vitamin A	IU	391.0	10.0
LIPIDS			
Saturated, total	g	0.767	0.030
Monounsat. total	g	0.419	0.016
Poly. total	g	1.141	0.045

Fresh radish sprouts vs. raw, white icicle garden radish..

Nutrient Content of Sprouted Seeds vs. Unsprouted Seed or Vegetable

Milligrams per 100 grams edible portion [30A].

	WATER	VIT C	VIT A	FAT
LENTIL	11.19	6.2	39.	0.96
SPROUTED	67.34	16.5	45.	0.55
RED PEA	11.95	1.5	50.	1.26
SPROUTED	89.78	36.0	712.	0.25
SOYBEAN	8.54	6.0	24.	19.94
SPROUTED	69.05	15.3	11.	6.70
MUNG	9.05	4.8	114.	1.15
SPROUTED	90.4	13.2	21.	0.18
RADISH	95.37	29.0	10.	0.10
SPROUTED	90.07	28.9	391.	2.53
GREEN PEA	11.7	1.5	107.	1.3
SPROUTED	62.7	10.4	166.	0.68

Line 1 of each group represents the unsprouted bean. Line 2 "SPROUTED" is the sprouted version of that food. Red pea, also known as China red pea, is the domestic version of the Japanese adzuki bean. Values here represent the mature plant grown in soil. The red pea has the advantage of developing an edible green leaf after 10-12 days growth. This is the reason for its high vitamin A and ascorbic acid (vitamin C). The other beans such as mung, were sprouted for 3-5 days without soil. "Radish" is the raw vegetable compared with radish sprouts.

Even NASA Knows

A seed sprouting system has been developed for the space shuttle as a source of fresh vegetables for astronauts on long space flights. Sprouts can be a potential source of living foods even in the micro-gravity environment of space. The self-contained sprouting system developed by the Johnson Space center and PhytoResource Research, Inc. pumped air, water and oxygen into small transparent 6 ounce plastic cups which are the standard containers for dehydrated food and drink mixes in the Space Shuttle. The sprouter added tiny amounts of water frequently because excess water tended to cling to the seeds through surface tension impeding the flow of oxygen and drowning the seeds. The kit also periodically deflated and reinflated the sealed cups to remove gaseous waste products and supply fresh oxygen. If the program expands (it is constrained by budget cuts), NASA may become a major promoter of sprouting! [12]

About the Data

Some values are for dry weight, some are for fresh produce. Mung sprouts, for example, contain 90.40 grams of water for every 100 grams of sprouts. Mung beans, on the other hand, contain only 9.05 grams of water per 100 grams of beans. Thus, when we compare the nutrient content of sprouts and beans, we must keep in mind that the sprouts are extremely diluted. The 3.04 grams of protein for mung sprouts seems much less than the 23.86 grams in the beans. However, 3.04 grams represents approximately 30% of the sprout's dry weight while the 23.86 grams represents approximately 91% of the bean's dry weight. Equalizing both sprout and bean to an ideal 100% dry weight model, the sprout would yield a calculated value of 31.66 grams of protein per 100 grams dry weight and the bean only 26.23. Since lab analyses of sprouts are not as plentiful as common foods, we lack dry weight studies on many nutrients and may be forced to interpret data accordingly. This mathematical calculation may prove different than a real dry weight analysis. However, the real analysis is also fraught with accuracy problems because many nutrients are either altered or lost by the dehydration process required for dry weight testing. Either way, we lack a perfect analysis of what we actually get when we eat live sprouts.

Although much of the data in these tables was derived from studies by the U.S. department of Agriculture Western Regional research laboratory, other sources were also used *(see resources p. 180.)*. Since sprouts are not all grown equal, the values presented could be more or less than those you can achieve in your kitchen. To your advantage, your personal control over quality may provide better nutrition than obtained in a laboratory and listed on these pages. In comparing data, keep in mind that the studies were not necessarily made from the same sample. Different mung beans, for example, may be used for the raw, cooked and sprouted studies. In addition, inconsistencies are created by different seed sources and qualities, different growing environments, processing techniques, lengths and conditions of storage, laboratories and different methods of extraction and analysis. Most critical of all, data will differ if a sprout is tested on the 3rd, 5th, 7th or 9 day of maturity. The various studies undoubtably tested on different days, but maturity and growing procedures were rarely reported.

List of Abbreviations and Measures

g	Grams	oz	Ounce
IU	International unit	quart	0.946 liter
kcal	Kilocalorie	quart	946.6 milliliters
mcg	Microgram	ounce	28.35 grams
mg	Milligram	pound	453.6 grams

Digesting Sprouted Beans

To Cook or Not to Cook?

Sprouts and raw foods are sometimes considered synonymous. One would not consider cooking a salad, for example. But our selection of sprouting seeds extends beyond the salad domain.

Sprouting seeds are catagorized according to those varieties that develop a green leaf and those that do not. The green, chlorophyll developing seeds are for salads and should be grown vertically, as is lettuce in your garden. Grains and beans are generally not chlorophyll developing and thus, for our purposes, do not need light in order to mature. These are mung, lentil, chick pea (garbanzo), green pea, soy, adzuki, red pea, pinto, navy and kidney bean. These beans are usually sprouted from 3 to 5 days in home sprouters and still look very much like beans with a tail on them. There is no metamorphosis of the bean as with alfalfa and clover, which transform themselves from legumes into a completely different entity--a green plant. Although sprouting makes the large beans easier to digest, increases their protein and lowers their starch, they are still primarily raw beans. Quantity and regularity of consumption is the caveat here. One should not *regularly* consume *large quantities* of raw beans or raw sprouted beans.

This is more of an issue for the bigger beans than it is for the smaller ones. Big beans such as soy, garbanzo, green pea, kidney, navy and pinto should be cooked until soft all the way through. Fortunately, sprouted beans need much less cooking than raw beans. This has two advantages: the sprouted bean offers us more nutrients and the reduced cooking destroys less of them. A good cooking method would be "low heat, long term cooking". Turn the flame on low, put on the cover and let simmer until done. Leave the lid ajar near the end of the cooking process to relieve escaping gases. Stir periodically and never let all the water cook out. Make sure the beans are soft throughout before eating. Although sprouting greatly reduces all of the bean's digestive inhibitors and toxins, cooking insures the job is complete.

Smaller size beans such as mung, lentil, adzuki, and red pea, can be eaten raw in larger quantities than their big bean brothers. This is especially true if their shoots are greater than 1 inch long. The longer the sprout, the easier they are to digest. But for maximum digestibility, they should be lightly steamed or wok sautéd whenever large quantities are consumed regularly. Cooking time is even shorter for these beans. Adzuki, its American sister the China red pea and its cousin the mung bean, can also be grown to the green stage. *(See p. 63.)* Once these beans develop green leaves like alfalfa and clover, they take on the qualities of lettuce. The greens can be consumed without cooking. Unfortunately, lentils, green peas, soybeans, garbanzos and other big beans are either not possible or not palatable to grow to the green stage. With the partial exception of lentils, these beans should be cooked for best digestion.

Grains such as wheat, rye, oat, millet, barley and corn are too hard to digest raw unless they are sprouted to the green or "grass" stage. Technically, grains are chlorophyll developing plants because they are all grasses. Grasses are, of course, green, but they are not salad foods...at least for humans. For cows and horses, they are haute cuisine! Grains are usually sprouted from 2 to 5 days in a sprout bag and yield a sprout that is 1 to 2 times the size of the berry. The grains can be dried and pulverized into flour or ground into sprout dough for making sprouted breads, cookies, crackers, etc. Soft wheat sprouts are relatively easy to digest and may be eaten raw as snacks or mixed with dried fruit in small quantities. Again, we do not normally consume raw grain and sprouted grain is not much different. It still needs some cooking to be completely digestible. Baking sprouted grain for sprout bread, however, can be accomplished at temperatures much lower than standard bread. Sprouted wheat dough usually bakes at 250°F. compared with 450°F. for common bread baking. Because these temperatures are so low, sprout bread can take as long as 3 hours to bake. The bread is dried as much as it is baked.

In summary, grains or big beans, should be cooked for optimum digestibility whenever consumed regularly or in quantity.

Cook these big bean sprouts:
   Sprouted soy, garbanzo, green pea, pinto, kidney, navy.
Lightly steam or sauté these if consumed regularly or in quantity:
   Sprouted mung, lentil, adzuki, red pea.
Make these into sprout bread or grass juice:
   Sprouted wheat, kamut, spelt, rye, soft wheat.

Natural Toxins In Beans
Are No Cause for Alarm

Until man duplicates a blade of grass, Nature can laugh at his so-called scientific knowledge.

Thomas A. Edison.

Many plants, fruits, vegetables, grains and beans contain natural toxins, enzymes and substances some of which may interfere with digestion. Speculation is that these chemicals function, at least in part, as a natural defense against bacterial, fungal, insect and perhaps animal predators.

Beans, for example, are famous for their gas producing effects. They contain substances which interfere with the action of trypsin, the major protein digesting enzyme. If the inhibitor is not denatured by sprouting or cooking, it can interfere with trypsin and thus the digestion of protein. This results in the bean's fame for flatulence. These inhibitors, however, are water soluble and a simple procedure reduces their gas producing properties: Soak the beans, pour off the soak water, cook them and pour off the cook water. Sprouting achieves the same results in the small beans like adzuki, red pea, mung and lentil, because of the soaking and daily rinsing routine. The germinating bean also reduces and eliminates the inhibitors because of the chemical and enzymatic changes during its growth [4]. Sprouting larger beans such as garbanzo, soybeans and green peas, also reduces and eliminates the trypsin inhibitors but because of their high starch content, they still need the catabolic action of cooking to make them fully digestible.

Another unfriendly natural agent in beans is phytic acid. Phytic acid is a form of phosphorus found mostly in beans. It binds with trace minerals such as zinc, manganese, and chromium. The germination of grains reduces phytic acid and even liberates phosphorous for the production of phospholipids such as lecithin [33]. This same mineral unavailability also occurs with calcium due to the interference of oxalic acid. Oxalic acid is found in seeds such as sesame and vegetables such as rhubarb, spinach and mushrooms. Both oxalic and phytic acids are soluble in water and are converted and eliminated during germination.

Do Natural Toxins Cause Cancer?

In the early 1980's, Bruce Ames a prestigious biochemist at the University of California at Berkeley, published a series of articles on natural toxins in plants. He described numerous substances found in common fruits, vegetables, grains and beans that when isolated and fed to monkeys and rodents had mutagenic effects. Ames developed the "Ames test for Mutagenicity" which provided a yardstick for measuring the toxicity of foods. Some substances were carcinogenic in reaction with proteins and fats during certain types of cooking procedures such as frying. Coffee, potatoes, tomatoes, black pepper and beans were among the many guilty foods. In fact, Ames espoused the opinion that natural plant toxins were a greater threat than man-made pesticides!

Included in the long list of guilty foods was alfalfa "sprouts". Alfalfa is, in fact, a tiny bean, the smallest member of the legume family. It and other legumes contain natural substances such as the trypsin inhibitors, phytic and oxalic acids mentioned above. The most controversial toxin in alfalfa beans is L-Canavanine. L-Canavanine is an analog of the amino acid arginine that is incorporated into protein in place of arginine. It is one of approximately 200 non-protein amino acids synthesized by plants [39]. In tests, monkeys fed alfalfa tablets containing L-Canavanine sulfate and alfalfa seeds, developed symptoms similar to systemic lupus erythematosus (SLE) [13]. Lupus, in man, is an auto-immune disease in which the body's natural defense mechanism turns against itself. It is marked by degenerative symptoms such as redness of the skin, lesions, arthritic pain and can be internal or external. Scientists have long searched for the cause of SLE although it is most often induced as a side effect of certain drugs. In vitro tests (in the test tube not the body), demonstrate that L-Canavanine disrupts the functioning of chromosomes which in turn skews the immune system [14,15]. This disruption appears to involve oxygen radicals generated as a response to L-canavanine because its toxic effects were neutralized by the addition of anti-oxidants [16].

Bean Sprout vs. Green Sprout. A Big Difference.

The incrimination of alfalfa sprouts in the studies on the canavanine-alfalfa-lupus connection is a distortion of the results and a confusion in terms between alfalfa seeds, alfalfa seedlings and alfalfa sprouts. None of the research actually involved alfalfa sprouts as they are typically consumed. Instead the monkeys, rodents and rabbits were fed biscuits made from alfalfa seeds as well as alfalfa meal from alfalfa hay and tablets containing high doses of L-canavanine sulfate. The thrust of the research was to explore the connection between the toxin and the disease. It was not a test of alfalfa sprouts and, in fact, "sprouts" played only a marginal role in 2 of the numerous studies done on this toxin. The research demonstrated a potential for this toxin to *reactivate* SLE in previously diseased monkeys. But the connection between alfalfa sprouts, as we typically consume them, and the disease was never studied nor proven.

The definition of alfalfa sprouts makes all the difference. A seedling is a germinated seed with a tail or shoot but no leaf. A mature sprout has shed its bean pod and evolved into a tiny green plant. For common alfalfa sprouts grown in a home environment, this takes approximately 1 week. The "sprouts" used in the research were 1-3 day old non-green seedlings which were then oven-dried to reduce their bulk. Forty percent of the monkey's diet consisted of this germinated seed for 7 months. No tests were done with mature, green alfalfa sprouts as you would purchase them in the produce market. They could not use "real" sprouts because they make too much bulk and would be an impossible amount for the monkeys to consume. Secondly, the more the seeds are germinated, the lower the concentration of canavanine. In fact, when the sprout matures, there is no trace of it at all [36]. Despite an intense diet that was 43% fat, 34%

carbohydrate and 23% protein [14] and was purified to consist of alfalfa seed, oven-dried germinated seed, seed biscuits and canavanine spiked alfalfa tablets, only about half of the monkeys in the two primary studies acquired lupus-like symptoms, the others showed no abnormalities [13]. The research proved that this kind of diet reactivated the syndrome in those monkeys who had it before, but was not universal in inducing the disease. "...The lupus like syndrome occurs only in a select number of monkeys given alfalfa seeds..." "One monkey died after 10 weeks of L-canavanine ingestion {L-canavanine sulfate at 2 percent}..."[13].

Much of the work on the alfalfa-canavanine-Lupus connection was driven by M. René Malinow. It started with his volunteering himself to eat large quantities of alfalfa seeds in an effort to lower blood cholesterol and prevent atherosclerosis. During the first 5 months of 1979, he ate 80 to 160 grams of ground alfalfa seeds daily in regimens that lasted 6 weeks at a time. His plasma cholesterol levels fell from a 218 to 130 mg per deciliter [40,41]. Although the cholesterol results were marvelously successful, there were side effects. Malinow developed auto-immune symptoms. He returned to normal after discontinuing his experimental diet, but his experience stimulated further work by him and others on the connection between L-canavanine and the lupus-like symptoms.

No one in good sense should eat a concentrated diet of raw alfalfa beans or any raw unsprouted beans. An alfalfa bean with a tail one inch long, is still a bean. Only when its growth reaches the first leaf division does it change into a baby green vegetable. This is the mature state of the young plant. The L-canavanine toxin is not present in the mature plant or in the cooked bean [37]. Even if it were, one would have to eat an enormous quantity of sprouts to get it. Canavanine represents 1.5% of the dry weight of alfalfa seed. Since fresh alfalfa sprouts are approximately 95% water (depending on the number of days growth), then the canavanine in the mature sprout would represent a 0.00075% concentration.[1] Even if this tiny amount were enough to cause trouble, the actual amount is even less. According to Emil J. Bardana, who worked along with Malinow

[1] 1.5% of 5% dry weight.

and another co-worker, Anthony Montanaro, "you'd have to eat a wheelbarrow full of alfalfa sprouts to get the dosage we fed the monkeys" [57].

☞ *When you grow alfalfa to the green stage, a metamorphosis takes place. It is no longer a legume, but a green plant. The toxin associated with legumes is not present in mature alfalfa.* ☜

In a personal interview with this author, Dr. Bardana stated that there is no basis to say that eating alfalfa sprouts would cause lupus or SLE. "I wouldn't discourage my lupus patients from eating alfalfa sprouts." The amount of sprouts you eat on a salad or a vegetable dish "isn't anywhere near the dose we gave the monkeys." The researchers could not use the alfalfa sprouts you find in the market because in order to achieve the dosage levels required, the bulk would be enormous and impossible to consume. All they could do was germinate the seed for a day or two and even then they had to oven-dry it to reduce the bulk. Only a portion of the diet consisted of this germinated seed because they needed the higher concentrations of canavanine from the ungerminated seed. Bardana lamented that they never received the funding from the NIH (National Institute of Health) to test real human dosage levels. The closest we have come to human testing is a study of two lupus patients in remission who took a daily dose of 15 and 8 alfalfa tablets representing a canavanine dose of approximately 0.27 and 0.15mg respectively. The authors, two clinical nutritionists from Rush University concluded: "It is still uncertain that these amounts ingested daily over months or years are able to reactivate SLE in humans" [56]. Since L-canavanine is also present in such high consumption, staple foods as garlic, onions and soybeans, it is still unproven that a normal diet of such foods does anything but good.

Some confusion over the number of days growth to maturity is understandable. Larger legumes like mung, lentil, soy and peas are all considered fully sprouted and mature with a 1½ inch tail. Under home sprouting conditions, this takes 4 to 5 days. It is wrong to assume that alfalfa is mature in the same time frame. The difference between alfalfa, its legume cousin clover and the other beans is that alfalfa is heliotropic. It transforms into a green plant while the others remain a bean with a tail. All heliotropic (green leafy) sprouts, mature when they reach their first leaf division and achieve a rich green color. This completes their metamorphosis from a bean into a vegetable and reaches its nutritional peak. Green sprouts should be treated like lettuce and eaten raw. Soybean and other big bean sprouts should be cooked or steamed to insure the elimination of any remaining trypsin inhibitors or other toxins not converted by sprouting and to increase digestibility. Eaten in this way, sprouts only promote health, not take it away.

As for mung and lentil sprouts, quantity is everything. Fully sprouted mung and lentil beans, in portions typically consumed in raw salads is completely healthful. Larger portions should be steamed for better digestion. Cook these sprouts only if you eat them regularly and in large quantities. Canavanine, phytic acid and trypsin inhibitors, are all water soluble and heat liable. Cooking neutralizes them [37]. Sprouting also converts and reduces them, that is why they can be consumed raw in respectable quantities. Mature green leafy sprouts can and should be eaten raw in any quantity. The greatest threat to health involving alfalfa and clover sprouts is the consumption of them when soggy and smelly. Sprouts that have "turned" are decaying and are loaded with toxins, fungi, unfriendly bacteria and ammonia. They are a greater threat to health than L-canavanine. Caution is also a must when juicing these sprouts. Intensive juicing regimes like the Gerson therapy, requiring 8-12 juice drinks per day, can concentrate toxins and inhibitors if immature sprouted beans are juiced. On the other hand, juicing of mature, green, clean and healthy alfalfa sprouts will have only the most cleansing and nourishing results. Never juice non-green alfalfa and clover sprouts, or raw mung, lentil, adzuki, big beans, red or green pea sprouts. Big bean sprouts such as soy and pea should be cooked as they have been by Asian and Latin peoples for centuries. These few tenets will keep your sprout diet safe and healthful. *(See To Cook or not to Cook, p. .)*

Natural Toxins Are Not New

Natural toxins are not a new threat to our health. Societies world-wide have been consuming them for thousands of years. Organic chemists have been characterizing such substances for over 100 years. Today, due to the availability of modern short-term tests for detecting mutagens, scientists are simply identifying more of them.

L-Canavanine belongs to a large family of natural plant toxins in common foods such as oxalic acid in rhubarb and spinach, phytic acid in beans, solanine in potatoes and tomatoes, strychnine in mushrooms, cyanide in the seeds of apples and apricots and aphlatoxin in peanuts and corn. Putting things in perspective, in Bruce Ames discussion of dietary carcinogens, the canavanine-alfalfa connection represents one paragraph of a seven page report on natural toxins. He finds many more formidable poisons to warn us about including the mutagens, toxins and carcinogens in cocoa, fava beans, mustard, cottonseed oil, tea, citrus fruit, mushrooms, celery, parsnips, figs, parsley, black pepper and oil of sassafras (root beer) to name a partial list. In fact, Ames finds numerous toxins in the most sacred of American foods--the morning cup of coffee.

One cup of coffee contains 250mg of the natural mutagen chlorogenic acid, highly toxic atractylosides....and about 100mg of caffeine which inhibits a DNA repair system and can increase tumor yield and cause birth defects at high levels in several experimental species [1].

If you are not willing to give up your coffee, how about forsaking your potato? Potatoes belong to the nightshade family which includes tomatoes, eggplants, peppers and tobacco. All members contain poisonous alkaloids. Potatoes contain solanine which occurs in all green parts of the plant and in the tuber itself especially if it is exposed to light long enough to turn green. Peppers contain atropine also known as belladonna. Tobacco contains the proven carcinogen nicotine, which when isolated is a powerful insecticide.

Common black pepper contains nearly 10% (by weight) piperine, Piperine is related to safrole which causes cancer in mice. Should we therefore deduce that black pepper, a condiment on nearly every dining table in America, causes cancer in humans? Aflatoxin is one of the most potent carcinogens known and just hearing its name is alarming to the public. It can be a contaminant in moldy bread, cheese, corn, peanuts and fruit, but it is extremely rare. Nitrosamines and nitroso compounds are suspected causes of stomach and digestive tract cancers. Beets, celery, lettuce, spinach, radish and rhubarb all contain 200 milligrams or more of nitrates (per 100 gram portion). Should we incriminate these common vegetables, consumed for thousands of years across multi-national and cultural borders because chemical components isolated within them have demonstrated mutagenic effects on rats?

Anti-Oxidants & Anti-Carcinogens

All right. Nature is not benign. Natural toxins do exist. But natural foods and particularly sprouts, also contain numerous beneficial enzymes, anti-oxidants and anti-carcinogens such as vitamin E, beta-carotene, selenium, super-oxide dismutase and ascorbic acid (vitamin C) that act as the body's defense mechanism against toxins whether natural or man-made.

Beta-Carotene is found in mature alfalfa sprouts and in all plants that contain chlorophyll. It is a very efficient free radical trap [17] and has demonstrated anti-carcinogenic activity in rats and mice [18]. Selenium significantly inhibits skin, liver, colon, and mammary tumors in experimental animals by a variety of carcinogens [19]. Glutathiones, rich in foods containing the sulfur amino acids, are major anti-oxidants and anti-mutagens and may even be effective against potent aflatoxins [20]. Vitamin C (ascorbic acid) was shown to be anti-carcinogenic in rodents treated with ultraviolet radiation and nitrite. Mushrooms like shitake contain the active polysaccharide compound lentinan. Lentinan stimulates interferon production. Interferon is a powerful anti-tumor agent [27].

☞ ☞ ☞ *We know that "free radicals" are the*
guilty party because chromosome breaks created in the presence
of L-Canavanine sulfate were prevented by the anti-oxidant
superoxide dismutase [16]. ☜ ☜ ☜

Raw and sprouted vegetables contain enzymes that oppose tumor growth. Tumors release enzymes called proteases which break down healthy tissue around the tumor and increase potential tumor growth. Inhibiting enzymes in live foods called protease inhibitors, block the actions of these proteases and the spread of the tumors. Sprouted seeds and beans, particularly soybeans and lima beans, are our finest dietary sources of these protective enzymes [23].

Flaxseeds and their young sprouts are one of our best dietary sources of the essential omega-3 fatty acids such as alpha-linolenic acid. Freshly sprouted 1-2 day flaxseeds provide an excellent source of this extremely unstable oil. Studies show that the omega fatty acids have an inhibiting effect on tumor growth [24]. Specifically, they decrease the synthesis of prostaglandins thus decreasing the migratory ability of tumor cells and metastasis [25].

Sprouts also show promise to help in the fight against breast cancer. Soybean sprouts are nature's finest source of plant isoflavones which are converted in our stomachs to isoflavone equol. High estrogen levels stimulate breast tumor growth, but research shows isoflavone equol to have excellent anti-estrogenic qualities similar to that of cruciferous vegetables [26].

In 1992, researchers at Johns Hopkins University Medical school isolated sulphoraphane, a compound found in broccoli and other brassica family vegetables. Sulphoraphane stimulates a cell's production of certain protective enzymes that resist tumor growth [9]. Studies of cancer patterns in the U.S. and abroad reveal strong statistical linkage between the consumption of raw vegetables and relative immunity to a variety of cancers. Researchers have long known that cells exposed to carcinogens respond by generating an assortment of highly effective enzymes that guard against malignant growth. They appear to work by bonding with the toxins and preventing their chemicals from reaching the cell's vulnerable genetic material. Then, they flush them from the body. The most effective enzyme stimulated by the sulphoraphane in cabbage family foods is called quinone reductase. Sulphoraphane, by the way, is related to mustard oil. Foods that contain sulphoraphane are cabbage, broccoli, kale, cauliflower, turnip, Chinese cabbage, collard greens, brussel sprouts and even non-cruciferous vegetables like carrots, green onions, chives and the sprouts of broccoli, kale, turnip, garlic, onion and Chinese cabbage.

Chlorophyll, one of the most basic nutritional elements in plants, is a well known blood purifier and, in fact, is similar in chemical structure to human hemoglobin. Numerous animal studies demonstrate that chlorophyll can be converted into hemoglobin. Alfalfa sprouts are one of our best dietary sources of earth grown chlorophyll. (Algae from lakes is highest.)

Alfalfa sprouts have also demonstrated a remarkable cholesterol reducing capacity. Studies in both humans and a wide selection of animals including dogs, rabbits, chickens, pigeons and pigs have shown a regression of atherosclerosis [40] and a considerable drop in the levels of serum cholesterol. Saponins in alfalfa appear to be responsible for lowering cholesterol and balancing the bile [41]. They create a sudsing action that prevents cholesterol and bile salts from being absorbed. Although there has been concern in the past about the toxicity of saponins, research showed positive results in the lack of toxicity of alfalfa saponins in monkeys and rats [42].

Enzymes are protein-like chemical agents that facilitate all life-building processes such as digestion, absorption and metabolism. The enzyme and anti-oxidant super-oxide dismutase, abundant in sprouts especially green sprouts like alfalfa, obstructs the free radical-canavanine-alfalfa pathology. In a 1980 report published in *Human Genetics*, chromosome breaks caused by free radicals were prevented by the anti-oxidant super-oxide dismutase [16]. In a 1993 study at the Indiana University School of Medicine, 78 female mice received a lethal dose of 580 rads of x-radiation designed to cause extreme free-radical activity. Half of the 23 placebo-fed mice died within 30 days. The remaining 55 mice were fed supplements made from wheat sprouts. All of them survived except one. Wheat sprouts are high in the pre-cursor enzyme that stimulates the body's manufacture of super-oxide dismutase [35].

Wheat sprouts have also demonstrated anti-mutagenic activity in mice and rats in three separate studies. Members of the flavonoid family, shaftoside and swertisine, both glycosides of apigenin appear responsible for the wheat sprouts' strong anti-mutagenic behavior [38]. The sprouts were not grown to the grass or green stage.

Perhaps because of their rapid germination and protein manufacture, sprouts are also rich sources of nucleic acids. Nucleic acids are the genetic keys to protein and tissue growth found in the cytoplasm, nucleus and chromosomes of cells. They resist cell mutation and promote healthy cell growth. These results indicate that sprouts have a profound effect on our ability to fend off free-radical induced diseases such as cancer and immune system disorders.

Now for the Real Carcinogens

Rather than isolating and attacking natural toxins in plants which are balanced by a multitude of enzymes and nutrients, perhaps we should turn our efforts to eliminating known carcinogens in our environment. Free oxygen radicals are caused by numerous dietary and lifestyle factors including medical drugs, air and water pollution, pesticides, alcohol, cigarettes, fried foods, smoked and barbecued foods, nitrates, even good old toast and coffee.

Charred meats and rancid fats should not be part of anyone's diet. The heating of proteins and fats creates a variety of DNA damaging agents [22]. So does the carmelization of sugars and amino acids visible on the browned ends and crust of common toasted bread. In fact, the amount of burnt and browned material in the human diet may be several grams per day. In comparison, a 2 pack-a-day smoker only takes in 500 mg of burnt material. Since they shorten their lives by an average of 8 years, what are we doing to our longevity by ingesting charred foods? How much does a resident of Los Angeles shorten his/her life by inhaling its severely polluted air? Alcohol, whose consumption is widespread in most cultures, has long been associated with cancers of the digestive tract as well as chromosome damage [28].

☞ ☞ ☞ *Lupus erythematosus is caused more by modern drugs than anything else.* ☜ ☜ ☜

Drugs are major carcinogens. Even lupus erythematosus, the disease that is the focal point of the L-canavanine-alfalfa controversy, is caused more by modern medicine than anything else. Drugs most frequently responsible are hydralazine, commonly prescribed for lowering blood pressure, procainamide, used to treat heart irregularities and isoniazid [34].

Perhaps the greatest irony of all is the use of powerful cancer-causing chemicals in the treatment of cancer itself. Information about the toxicity of these drugs is widely known. In the *Physicians Desk Reference*, available in any library or doctor's office, the top 10 chemotherapy drugs used in the USA all have cancer as a listed side effect. In fact, depending on how you interpret the statistics, more cancer patients die of the chemotherapy than of the cancer. The medical statisticians count these deaths as a success for chemotherapy because the patient did not die of cancer. Few people know that chemotherapy drugs are not FDA approved. They are legally administered under the *Rule of Probable Cause*. The "Rule of Probable Cause" states that experimental drugs may be used if the side effect of the drug is no worse than the end effect of the disease. In fact, every chemotherapy bottle is stamped "For Experimental Use Only" and the patient must sign a release before the doctor will prescribe or administer it. [29,34]

☞ ☞ ☞ *FOOD IS INNOCENT UNTIL PROVEN GUILTY.* ☜ ☜ ☜

Science Or Truth?

In early 1991, two scientists from the University of British Columbia in Vancouver, published a widely publicized study of nearly 1,000 persons which indicated that left-handed persons died at an earlier age than right-handed persons. Needless to say, many people were frightened. But in 1993, researchers at Harvard and the National Institute of Aging studied 3,800 persons and determined that righties and lefties died at exactly the same rate. The authors of the Boston study strongly criticized the first group's interpretation of their data. These two similar studies with opposite results describe one of the problems of scientific research: data may have more than one interpretation.

☞ ☞ ☞ *Data can have more than one interpretation. Just to identify a substance as a carcinogen does not mean that typical consumption of foods containing it will cause cancer.* ☜ ☜ ☜

Science is always authoritative, but does it always represent the truth? Stories in the press about natural toxins are alarming to consumers, especially those who make the effort to eat a natural diet. Making matters worse, many health professionals who have neither the time nor skill to investigate further, accept all research as fact and lend their credibility to it. To say that alfalfa sprouts contain a toxin that generates free radicals which in turn causes abnormal cell development and thus potential cancer is, in itself, factual. But the interpretation is not necessarily true. This process of exaggerating fact to where it is no longer relevant is called disinformation. Yes, we can prove that metal is heavier than water, but should we then conclude that all metal boats must sink? One could easily devise a metal boat that does sink and publish a study proving it. That would be an example of bad science. When it comes to food, science loves to take it apart and examine it. But food is innocent until proven guilty. Isolating components, concentrating them into tablets and feeding them to monkeys or rodents, may have little to do with our dinner salad. Ames himself recognizes that just to identify a substance as a carcinogen does not mean that typical consumption of foods containing it will cause cancer.

*The quantification of risk poses a major chal-
lenge....Carcinogens differ in their potency in rodents by
more than a millionfold and the levels of particular carcinogens to which humans are exposed can vary more
than a billion fold. Extrapolation of risk from rodents to
humans is difficult for many reasons, including the longevity difference, anti-oxidant factors and the probable
multi-causal nature of most human cancer.* - B. Ames [1]

Misdirected Sensationalism

It is unfortunate how quickly panic spreads when fear is promul-
gated through negative press. If we focus on the cyanide in apple
seeds, we discard a perfectly nourishing and beneficial fruit. The
real misfortune of disinformation is to be sucked into the sensation-
alism of a low gravity issue and ignore the greater menace to our
health from threats such as fried foods, high fat diets, smoking, alcohol consumption, irradiation, preservatives, synthetic sweeteners,
modern medicines and pesticides, to name a few.

☞ ☞ ☞ *Not all natural toxins are bad. The dosage can change
a toxin's complexion from menace to cure.* ☜ ☜ ☜

Simply put, not all natural toxins are bad. Many poisons are
sources of important medicines. Strychnine, the toxin in mushrooms
is used to make medicines for the central nervous system and to
make the homeopathic remedy nux vomica. Atrxopine from peppers
is used to make the remedy belladonna used for fevers. The dosage
of a particular poison can change its complexion from menace to
cure. Too much uric acid, for example, may cause gout. But uric
acid is also a strong anti-oxidant and an insufficient amount in our
bloodstream increases the potential for lung cancer [1].

With all the panic about natural toxins, it is ironic that a certain level of pollution is legally allowed in our food. In its manual *Food Defect Action Levels*, the FDA allows a seven-ounce glass of tomato juice to contain up to 20 fly eggs. A one-pound box of macaroni can have up to nine rodent hair fragments; a pound of frozen broccoli can have 276 aphids; 3.5 ounces of apple butter can have up to five whole insects and a pound of cocoa beans can have up to 10mg of rodent feces. Were these facts to become known, they would probably frighten and disgust consumers more than free-radicals, L-canavanine or the many other natural toxins present in plants.

DON'T DOUBT THE SPROUT!

Broccoli Sprouts Prevent Cancer

In a 1997 study by John Hopkins University scientists, broccoli contains glucoraphanin, a chemical that, when eaten, is converted by the body into sulforaphane—the strongest natural inducer of the body's own enzymes against carcinogens. According to Paul Talalay, Ph.D. the Hopkins pharmacologist: "In animals and human cells, we have demonstrated, unequivocally, that this compound can substantially reduce the incidence, rate of development and size of tumors." The scientists found that broccoli sprouts contain a concentration of glucoraphanin that is up to 50 times greater than the mature broccoli we buy at the grocer. The sprouts raise the levels of protective enzymes that seem to work on many kinds of precancerous cells, although statistics link broccoli mainly to a lowered risk for colon cancer. The National Cancer Institute has funded several human studies of the sprouts.

Broccoli sprouts: An exceptionally rich source of inducers of enzymes that protect against chemical carcinogens. By Fahey JW, Zhang Y, Talalay P. Proc Natl Acad Sci U S A 1997 Sep 16;94(19):10367-10372.

EARTH & WATER

It takes organic life to develop and sustain organic life. This is a basic law of the organic world, a law that is instinctively recognized by all life save the civilized human. - J. A. Cocannouer.

PESTICIDES
At Last, The Beginning Of The End

In the early 1940's, farmers were experiencing crop losses of 5%-7% due to pests. Because of the push for productivity during the war, that amount of loss was considered unacceptable; thus pesticide use became widespread. Some of the chemicals derived from chemical warfare research were applied to crops as a solution. By 1947, everybody used them. Today, some 40 years later, America soaks its crops with two billion pounds of herbicides, insecticides, fungicides and other toxic chemicals costing between 1 and 2 billion dollars each year. In fact, most of our common foods, fruit, vegetables, grain products, even milk, eggs, poultry and meat, have residues of chemicals which in high doses cause cancer in laboratory animals. Some of our imported foods, which make up an increasingly larger percentage of what we put on our dinner plates, are treated with agri-chemicals which have been outlawed in the United States. A recent study by the U.S. Government Accounting Office found that up to 8.2% of imported produce contains hazardously high pesticide residues. Ironically, many of these chemicals are manufactured by U.S. companies and sold to third world and other countries from whom we import it. Where do these chemicals go? They become part of our ecosystem, polluting our air, soil and water.

Meanwhile, the bugs are winning. Dozens of species of insects have mutated and become immune to chemicals. Farmers suffer economic extinction in part because of the high cost of pesticides. And they have suffered physically with a higher demographic rate of sarcoma and lymphoma cancers due pesticide exposure. The damage pesticides have caused our national health--in personal illness and environmental pollution--is just now becoming evident to the average consumer. Ironically, in 1987, the United States Dairy Association did a study and found that crop loss due to pests was about 7%--the same as 40 years ago!. What have we accomplished?

Legal Doesn't Mean Safe

Unfortunately, the EPA's standards for "safe" pesticide levels were established in the 1960's and were based on the diet of an average adult. Recently the National Resources Defense Council (NRDC) completed a major study that analyzed 8 pesticides and found that cancer risks to children were several hundred times greater than the EPA "safe levels" and could effect their neurological and behavioral development. And there are so many delays in the regulation and monitoring of pesticides in food, that by the time pesticide contamination is detected, much of the food has already been sold and eaten.

Thank God for Apple Pie

Taking apples away from Americans is like robbing rice from the Chinese. But the pesticide Alar, used on our apples, plucked a string that resonated through America's bellies--a note of fear. The American consumer rebelled and the apple industry soured with a 50 million dollar drop in sales. At approximately the same time, arsenic-laden grapes from Chile arrived on our grocery shelves and underscored the dangers of chemically treated foods. Opinion polls now show that 77 percent of the American public believes that pesticides present a serious health hazard. Ironically, Alar, the trade name for the growth regulator Daminozide made by Uniroyal, is not nearly as dangerous as some of its pesticide cousins. Nevertheless, the apple industry, forseeing another $50 million dollar loss by the end of the year, surrendered to consumer pressure and "voluntarily" voted to stop using Alar in the Fall of 1989.

Change is coming. Agriculture must break its ties with the chemical industry and get out of the poison business. The federal government should supply farmers with financial and educational help and other incentives to switch to safer farming techniques such as Integrated Pest Management, bio-dynamic and organic farming. These techniques have been used for years, but farmers lack the skills, educational support and financial ability to weather the initial costs of making such a transition.

California growers are already experimenting with chemical-free growing techniques. The Federal Environmental Protection Agency classifies more than 70 of the currently licensed 360 pesticide ingredients as potential carcinogens. But farm groups insist that the only way to maintain current volumes and prices is with pesticides. Tests by the Florida Department of Agriculture and Consumer Services show that 69% of Florida grown produce contained traces of pesticides and 2.5% exceeded federal standards. Two pesticides, Maneb and Mancozeb, are among the most important chemicals used by Florida growers, yet their residues create a cancer risk 20 times greater than the established federal limit. About half of the nation's supply of winter vegetables are grown in Florida. Our solution has always been: Support organic farming, participate in community supported agricultures, buy locally and. . .grow sprouts!

A Brief Glossary Of The 12 Most Infamous Agricultural Chemicals

Chemical	*Description*
CAPTAN	Fungicide used on strawberries, apples, cherries, grapes, peaches, watermelon.
MANCOZEB	Fungicide used on tomatoes, potatoes and apples.
ALDICARB	Insecticide used on potatoes.
CHLORDANE	Insecticide. Potatoes 1948-1978. Banned in U.S.
PERMETHRIN	Lettuce, cabbage.
ENDOSULFAN	Insecticide. Apples, bananas, cantaloupes, cauliflower, celery.
LINDANE	Insecticide. Corn.
PARATHION	Insecticide. Broccoli, peppers, cherries, peaches.
METHAMIDOPHOS	Insecticide. Cantaloupes.
DIELDRIN	Insecticide. Corn, cucumbers, carrots. 1949-1974. Banned in U.S.
DDT	Insecticide. Carrots, potatoes. 1945-72. Banned in U.S.
PERMETHRIN	Insecticide. Cabbage, lettuce, tomatoes.

Foods Whose Samples Contained The Highest % Of Pesticide Residues

STRAWBERRIES	63%
PEACHES	55%
CELERY	53%
CHERRIES	52%
CUCUMBERS	51%
BELL PEPPERS	49%
TOMATOES	45%
SWEET POTATOES	37%
CANTALOUPES	34%
GRAPES	34%
LETTUCE	32%
APPLES	29%

What You Can Do

1) Buy organically-grown produce or support IPM grown produce. At least buy locally grown produce. Support local farmers.

2) Wash produce with soap and rinse thoroughly. Water is insufficient since most chemicals are not water-based. A detergent is necessary but even so only some of the surface pesticide will be removed.

3) Let your local farmers, supermarkets and grocery stores know of your desire to eschew all foods grown with pesticides or processed with synthetic chemical additives.

For more information about pesticides and how you can help, *see resources, p. 181.*

Pure Water
for You & Your Plants

Pure Water is Your Birthright

In the 1970's, many of us assumed that only the big cities had a water pollution problem. Today, with acid rain, ground water pollution, Chernobyl, and PCB's found in the Antarctic ice, we are all a little better educated. Of the 300,000 toxic waste sites in the U.S., the EPA has targeted 1,000 as their "priority" clean-up sites. The only real solution must include action on an individual level. That means--at our tap. We must make sure our cooking and drinking water is safe. Buying gallon jugs of spring water from far away places, year after year, is not economical, convenient or reliable. Federal regulations only require bottlers to test for a handful of the hundreds of known chemical contaminants. Water that is not sold across state lines is not even regulated by the FDA.

Using Pure Water for Rinsing Sprouts

Pure water is always recommended in both the soaking and rinsing stages. All the external food these young plants receive is contained in that water. If you use municipally treated water that is contaminated with fluoride and chlorine by-products (both fluoride and chlorine are added to most city water supplies), then you are essentially polluting a food that was organic and chemical-free to begin with. A good water filter is the easiest way to clean your water. But if you purchase spring water by the jug or own a water distiller, here are some techniques for watering your sprouts.

The soaking stage is easy. Just fill the jar with your pure water, add your seeds or beans and let sit. After soaking, transfer the seeds to the sprout bag and rinse the bag twice daily. Fill a pot with good water, then dip and swish the bag in it. Massage the sprouts under water so the roots will not hook into the walls of the bag.

When sprouting salad greens in a vertical sprouter, use a watering can with a sprinkler head. Hold the can high above the basket so that gravity will maximize the water flow rate to the seeds. The greater the water pressure during rinsing, the better the cleaning. Your rinsing is more than just a process of supplying water for the sprouts to drink, but also cleans them from invasions by mold and other bacteria.

Once the sprouts are 3-5 days old and have established anchors into the weaves of the basket, you can use the immersion method of rinsing in lieu of the sprinkler can. Fill up your sink or a basin with good water and dip the baskets in. Let them soak for 2-3 minutes, then remove and drain. Once the sprouts are tightly ensconced in their bamboo home, you can invert the basket and swish it around. This allows hulls which had fallen to the bottom of the basket to make their way out the top and down the drain. But never invert unless you are sure your sprouts are firmly anchored, less your sprouts fall down the drain, too.

Reusing Rinse Water

If you are buying spring water, then water is precious. This may tempt you to reuse the same rinse water twice. However, only reuse the water if it is clean. If it is cloudy or dirty, throw it away. Dirty water transfers bacteria cleaned from the first batch to the second.

Distilled Water & Sprouts

Distilled water is sterile. This is not a judgment against it since it is the preferred water for many purposes, but it is not ideal for sprouts. Sprouts drink in vitamins and minerals from the water and sterile water does not have any. If you own a water distiller for your own drinking purposes, we recommend modifying it for use with sprouts. Simply remineralize your distilled water by adding half a teaspoon of rice or other grain (wheat, rye, oat, millet, barley) per gallon of distilled water. The minerals and vitamins from the grains transfer to the water by osmosis, enlivening it and creating your own home-made mineral water. Keep this water refrigerated if storing for longer than 3 days and do not add more than the prescribed amount of grain or your mineral water will ferment. This water is perfect for people as well as plants.

How To Choose

A Water Purifying Device

Water is the most insidious poison in our diet. It is sad; it is ironic, but it is true. Water, our most vital ingredient next to air, has become so badly adulterated from environmental pollution that no stream, no river, no well, no reservoir escapes contamination. It is a sad comment on our society and the modern age that citizens must live in fear that the drinking water may harm them.

Citizens of New Orleans, for example, live at the end of what is probably the nation's most polluted waterway, the Missouri-Mississippi system and have the highest cancer rate in the nation. Philadelphians had their drinking water monitored from 1968-1978 and learned that their unusually high cancer fatalities was linked to different chemical polluters on the Delaware and Schuylkill rivers. Residents along the Chesapeake Bay (including Washington, D.C.) watch the Bethlehem Steel plant pour 300 million gallons of water containing oil, cyanide, and other dangerous chemicals into their river each day. And thousands of tons of chemicals were dumped at the infamous Love Canal in Niagra Falls, N.Y. among them at least 60 pounds of 2,4,5-T Dioxin. This synthetic chlorinated hydrocarbon is so potent that it is carcinogenic in parts per trillion!

The Pollutants

Pollutants like Dioxin, PCB's, pesticides, petrochemicals, and other industrial wastes are so insidious that they never break down in the environment and attempts to dump them frequently fail with leakage escaping into the ground water.

Midwest smokestacks belch up 27 million tons of sulfur dioxide and 21 million tons of nitrogen oxide into the air each year. These pollutants come down on the Eastern seaboard and Canada as acid rain, snow, dew, and fog creating polluted reservoirs, watersheds, dead lakes (no fish), damaged crops, and forests of stunted trees. Scientists unanimously agree that acid rain was the gravest environmental problem of the 80's and it is not getting better. In Colorado, one monitoring station reported a four-fold increase in acid rain since 1975, and a recent fog in Los Angeles had the acid content of lemonade.

Radioactive waste products are contaminating our water supply from atomic power plants, military weapons, and new medical technologies. Originally, barrels of these materials were dumped in the ocean 20 plus years ago. Because they are leaking and affecting aquatic life, the federal government is establishing permanent underground dumps in the continental U.S. starting in 1998. (Your own state may be one of the lucky ones selected.) By then nearly 70,000 metric tons of nuclear waste will be piled up in spent fuel pools by the nations 80 operating nuclear power plants alone.

If this isn't enough to make you sick, then maybe some of the more common pollutants will. Asbestos, nitrates, sodium, fluoride; heavy metals such as cadmium, lead, arsenic, mercury; common minerals such as sulfates, phosphates, aluminum; chlorine and chlorine by-products, chloroform, THM's; E. coli bacteria and giardia cysts; and hundreds of other multi-syllabled organic chemicals.

Mechanical Purifiers

Mechanical filters are almost all made of charcoal. Activated charcoal has long been famous for its odor and taste absorption properties. But the simplest of these filters, do very little more and in fact will breed bacteria in their warm moist environment.

Fortunately, space age techniques have allowed the creation of highly compressed carbon blocks. These carbon blocks are so dense that their microscopic pores are smaller than a red blood cell. This eliminates bacteria and provides superb purification. These devices are called purifiers, not just filters, due to their bacteria removing capabilities. In addition, their charged cellulose-cotton outer shell electro-kinetically absorbs particles too small for removal by mechanical straining.

The main advantages of these units is that they provide instant pure water at the turn of the faucet and allow the healthful, dissolved minerals in water to remain. Because they are mechanical devices, they use no energy and are inexpensive to maintain. Cartridges are rated at 500 gallons and have to be replaced an average of 1 to 2 times per year depending on volume of use and the condition of your water. The cost of replacing a cartridge averages from 6 to 7 cents per gallon.

Purifiers remove bad odor, color, taste, rust, dirt and scale, algae; all hydrocarbons including chlorine and chlorine by-products (THM's); pesticides such as DDT, EDB; over 100 cancer causing chemicals like TCE, harmful pathogenic bacteria such as E. Coli and Giardia cysts; toxic metals such as lead, cadmium, mercury, arsenic, asbestos, and turbid suspended matter. In essence they restore your water to its original pristine condition. They are weak in removing inorganic chemicals such as nitrates, fluorides and sodium. If these pollutants are of major concern to you, then you ought to consider a water distiller.

Distillers

Distillers are the oldest and still the most reliable means of water purification. Rain is a natural distillation process and distillers mimic that process. Water is first boiled into steam, then the steam is captured and condensed back into water. During the transformation of liquid to gas to liquid, anything with a modest molecular weight is removed. This would include the broadest range of elements since all pollutants, even radioactivity (from radioactive metals), has a molecular weight. The weak spot of a distiller, however, lies in the removal of low molecular weights--mostly gases. This is one of the factors that distinguishes a good distiller from a bad one.

Distillers have not been as popular as mechanical filters for a few reasons. (1) They cost more than filters. (2) They are relatively inconvenient because they take a couple of hours to make a gallon of water. (3) The public has been uncertain about drinking water without mineral or other life forms. It has been called "dead" water. There is a controversy as to whether sterile water is "healthy" or safe to drink.

After the purity of your distilled water is assured, through the integrity of the design and laboratory and consumer reviews, there are other considerations. You will want to know how much electricity the machine uses to make a gallon of water and how much coolant water it wastes to make one gallon of good water; how does it eliminate gases and low molecular weights; how long does it take to make one gallon; what materials is it made of; what is the warranty; how big or small is it; how is it hooked up; how often does it need cleaning and how easy is it to clean; does it provide its own reservoir; how convenient is it to operate and will it interfere with the use of your sink; and finally, how much does it cost?

Distillers can be expensive. They can range in price from as low as $225 to $1500 for household use. The more expensive units are not necessarily the purest. More often, they produce a higher volume of water, are more automated, and faster. Select a distiller which meets the needs of your household now and in the future. If two people average 1 to 1 ½ gallons of cooking and drinking water per day, a low output distiller would be adequate. However, since a distiller is a lifetime purchase, you may wish to plan ahead. Don't be fooled by advertising claims that a machine will output umteen gallons per day. You will not want to run your appliance all day. Choose one that will adequately fill your needs in less than half a day.

Purity is, of course, the primary concern. You do not want to make a large investment in a machine that eliminates only 95% of the pollutants. All distillers will at least do that. Even sophisticated carbon purifiers will do that. You want to achieve a 99.9%+ removal of contaminants. As mentioned before, the weak spot of a distiller is in the removal of gases and low molecular weight pollutants. A good distiller can do this many ways. It can, first, pre-boil the water for an extended period of time to vent most of the gaseous pollutants, or it may vent it through use of a fan, or an expanded surface area design which allows maximum aeration. In addition, some machines are actually combination units which include carbon filters in their design. This provides the best of both worlds since charcoal is known for its absorption of gases and low molecular weight organic pollutants. The filters are installed either before or after the water is distilled and are not subject to the bacteria problems of filters used alone. This makes for a superb marriage and is probably the safest route to take in todays world where pollutants are so broad and complex.

Size and hook-up are very important. You do not want your new purchase to turn into a monster in your kitchen. Some distillers hook up to the faucet prohibiting use of your sink. The hot waste water unpleasantly steams up your kitchen on a summer's day and the hoses require that you have adequate space near the sink. Some units are designed without attention to size and are as big as 4 feet tall. Others are designed compact and are as small as a large coffee pot. The best option would be to have one that can be mounted on the wall alleviating a counter space traffic jam and hooks directly to your water line.

Because distillers use energy, you want to be sure you get one that is energy efficient. Check how many watts it uses and how many hours it takes to make a gallon. Then determine how many watts are used per hour and thus how much it costs to operate per hour. Since this is your only maintenance expense, it can, over the years, turn a distiller with a low purchase price into a very expensive machine. If your distiller is water cooled (most are), then you will want to know how many gallons of water is wasted in manufacturing one gallon of pure water. Some distillers can waste as much as 6 gallons of water to make 1 gallon of pure water.

The materials used in a machine will have a great affect on its price. 100% stainless steel machines will be the most expensive. These units, which have intricate parts made of stainless steel, will be more expensive than those that substitute with plastic or aluminum in places where the purity of the water will not be compromised. If you are buying a machine with plastic parts, make sure they are using high quality, distiller tested plastic. In todays world, plastic means many things. Some space age plastics are nearly as strong as steel and are a far cry from the water jugs you buy in the supermarket. That kind of plastic is so soft it sometimes imparts a plastic taste to your water and is unsafe. The bottom line is: does it end up in the drinking water? If you are suspicious, check the lab reports.

The cost of your unit will also depend on the degree of automation which has a lot to do with convenience of use. Some distillers do nothing without you. If you are gone when the unit dries up, it will not shut itself off. And if it does not have its own reservoir, you have to collect the water in bottles, making sure to come back in time before the bottle overflows. You can overcome this by getting a 5 gallon bottle, but that takes up space in your kitchen, requires regular sterilization and a special dispenser to pump out the water. It can be a headache to make distilled water. A completely automated unit, however, turns itself on and shuts itself off. It has its own reservoir, sterilizes the water regularly, and after installed, never requires your attention for its daily operation. A manual unit requires that you fill it up with water each time you use it. You must remember to calculate your water needs. Most people prefer to do this only once a day.

Finally a word on the health benefits of drinking distilled water: no water is purer. If purity is your primary concern, then this is the water for you. The minerals in natural water are available from fresh fruits and vegetables, seafoods, grains and juices. It would take approximately 100 glasses of spring water to equal the amount of calcium in one glass of fresh carrot juice. However, if you feel your diet is not adequate, you may remineralize your distilled water by adding mineral tablets (available at health food stores) or just a few grains. Six grains of rice, for example, will mineralize 1 gallon of distilled water.

Make the choice that best suits you, but do make the choice to drink pure water. *(See also Resources p. 181.)*

Composting

Develop A Sense Of Humus!

The fall season's foliage is beautiful whether on the trees or fallen on the lawn. But it is a disgraceful sight to see them lined up along the roadside in plastic garbage bags.

Leaves are not garbage. No one should be throwing away yard debris. Approximately 20% of this country's solid waste stream is yard and garden waste. Grass clippings, leaves, weeds, trimmings, twigs, etc. do not belong in a municipal landfill. They contain rich resources of nitrogen, phosphorous, potassium and other nutrients which when composted will become a valuable plant food for your garden next season. To entomb them in a polyethylene bag for 300-500 years is an environmental tragedy. In one action we are both over-burdening our landfills and depleting our soil. Soil erosion and depletion is a national agricultural problem, yet we still pursue the misguided habit of sending vital plant resources away in a garbage truck.

How And What To Compost

Any serious gardener knows the value of composting. Preparation for next summer's garden starts in the fall. But even if you only mow your lawn and rake leaves, composting should be part of the job. A compost is like a sandwich of different materials:

> *Grass Clippings*
> *Mulched Leaves*
> *Twigs, Weeds and Yard Waste*
> *Kitchen Scraps, misc.*

Kitchen waste includes all fruit and vegetable trimmings and peels, tea bags, egg shells (crushed), coffee grounds, bread, meat or fat but no bones. Keep a separate holding bucket in your kitchen for scraps and transfer them to the composter every other day. Even miscellaneous items such as hair clippings and fire place ashes (cold) can be added to your compost.

The smaller the pieces the faster they decompose, so don't throw half a pineapple straight into the compost. Chop it up first. Do the same for banana peels, grapefruit skins, etc. The same goes for leaves. When mulched, they decompose in weeks rather than months. Chopping produces a better quality compost with a finer texture.

Friendly aerobic soil microbes and worms do the rest of the work with an occasional lift of the pitchfork on your part. Mixing the different layers of the compost aerates the batch, spreads the microbes and distributes the nutrients. Grass clippings, for example, are high in nitrogen while foliage is rich in carbon. The subsequent oxygenation of your compost materials speeds up decomposition and also eliminates odors. Compost starters are available if you are just beginning. They supply microbes and enzymes to stimulate the process much the same way as a yogurt starter helps to develop the first batch of yogurt. Manure is an excellent starter. Once you get it going, it is mostly self-perpetuating.

Air, Temperature & Moisture

These three elements are essential to making a successful compost. A composter should have vents on side walls and preferably even a trench under a slotted floor to allow air circulation underneath. Temperatures in an active compost can range from 105°F. to 140°F. which kills off weed seeds and harmful disease bearing organisms. Moisture is necessary for micro-organisms to reproduce and decomposition to occur, so keep your compost damp. The walls of the compost prevent evaporation and the top cover prevents drenching from rain and snow.

Building A Composter

Basically a composter is a box with good ventilation and a door or open end for access. Nothing fancy is required. Four pressure treated posts ($12) and a roll of 1 inch mesh chicken wire ($8 for 25 feet) will do. Use a tarp or a 4 x 8 sheet of outdoor rated plywood (½ inch thick, $16) as a roof. Allow one end of the mesh to be hooked but not nailed so it can be peeled back for easy access. Wood pallets, used for storing and shipping freight, can serve as a floor or even as walls. (Available at nurseries, wood, hardware stores or commercial shippers. Sometimes free.) For a fancier box, use pressure treated Living Lattice (usually used as an apron around the bottom half of porches and decks) as your four walls, again supported by four posts. A 4 x 8 sheet of lattice costs $17.

Winter Composting

Of course, the warm seasons are the best time to compost. Although there will be little activity in your compost during the very cold weather, you should continue feeding kitchen scraps--they will freeze. After the Spring thaw, there will be plenty of garden waste from Spring clean-up to mix with it. Finished compost, by the way, stores well all Winter long.

It's Organic!

Compost is the basis of a sound organic gardening and soil management. Compost delivers nutrients to the plants in a soluble form that they can readily absorb. Compost grown fruits and vegetables are healthier, more flavorful, more disease resistant and, of course, free of synthetic fertilizers and chemical pesticides. Finished compost can mature as fast as 4-6 weeks in the Summer and will have a dark brown loam, a crumbly texture and an earthy aroma.

Spare the landfill of the leaves and the rest of your garden waste. Rejuvenate your soil instead with your *Free* supply of organic fertilizer for a more reproductive garden and a healthier environment.

Fresh garlic chives are 12 day old chives, but pack a garlic punch.

Baby sunflower sprouts grow 6–7 inches tall and mature in 8–9 days. They have a hearty spinach-like texture but have twice the protein of spinach and four times more protein than common lettuce.

The

Seasoned Sprouter

Growing Soil-Free
Wheatgrass, Buckwheat and Sunflower

Wheatgrass, buckwheat, and sunflower seeds are traditionally sprouted in soil. However, by using a larger, heavy-duty, wide-weave bamboo basket the root systems of these plants will adapt themselves to the basket enabling the seedlings to grow. This means you can now enjoy these hearty sprouts without the time contraints and hassle of gardening in soil.

First, make sure you choose the right seeds. For growing wheatgrass, choose hard red winter, hard spring wheat or Kamut Egyptian wheat berries. Some stores do not know the difference between these varieties, others do not offer a choice. Simply ask for *hard wheat* berries. Do not use soft wheat, however. Soft wheat is lighter in color, lower in protein and gluten and is generally not used for growing wheatgrass since it is not as nutritious or hardy. Soft wheat berries are used for sprouted pastries and rejuvelac. For buckwheat lettuce, use raw, black, unhulled buckwheat. Buckwheat seed for sprouting has a black outer shell and is not suitable for cooking. Do not use buckwheat groats or kasha. Buckwheat groats have been hulled and kasha has been hulled and roasted. Neither is suitable for sprouting. For growing baby sunflower greens, use the small black oil sprouting grade seeds in-the-shell. Common striped confectionery sunflower seeds make tall, large sprouts, however, they yield a sparse crop because of their size and require manual removal of the shells. Although they are delicious, this extra labour makes them impractical. Try to obtain organic seeds whenever possible.

These sprouts are so big and hardy and require the use of strong, open weave sprouters. Because of this, small size vegetable seeds like alfalfa, clover, radish, cabbage, turnip, mustard, kale, rapeseed, etc. cannot be grown in the same sprouter. They fall right through the open weave.

How to Begin

1) Measure 6 tablespoons of any of the three seeds and soak in 16 oz of pure water. Stir well. This is especially important because sunflower seeds tend to float. After 10-12 hours of soaking, pour the seeds into the basket and let drain.

From here on, the sprouting procedures are the same as Alfalfa and the other small vegetable seeds, except these 3 seeds take longer to grow. Here are the steps in review:

2) Keep your basket at an angle for a few minutes until the water stops dripping.

3) Rinse at least twice a day with cold water. Use a shower spray instead of the hard flush of a faucet. Do not use a mister or atomizer. Good thorough rinsing and draining avoids most sprouting problems.

4) House the basket in a soft-plastic or rigid greenhouse tent. Create a large bubble of air in the plastic to ensure adequate air circulation. The greenhouse should look like a tent or a dome. Tuck the open end loosely under the basket. It does not have to be airtight. Your greenhouse is strong enough to stand up on its own.

5) The sprouter should remain in the greenhouse tent at all times except when rinsing. It retains moisture, maintains temperature, and allows light, including the valuable ultraviolet rays, to penetrate. *(See p. 48.)*

6) Keep in a shaded area during the first 4 days, then move to a bright area. Avoid direct sunlight, especially in warm weather. If too hot, temperatures in the greenhouse tent can climb to over 100° degrees and spoil your crop.

7) After the fourth day, or as soon as the sprouts have anchored themselves in the basket, you may bathe your sprouts by immersing the sprouter in a basin of pure water, even turning it upside down. The hulls will easily fall out. This cleans and rinses the sprouts at the same time. Make sure your sprouts are firmly rooted before trying this.

8) Harvest in 9-12 days.

Harvesting Buckwheat, Sunflower & Wheatgrass

These sprouted greens are ready to eat in 9-12 days. They have the longest and most virile root systems plus the largest hulls. For this reason, they require a special harvesting technique.

Grab a 1 inch bundle of sprouts about half way down their stalks. Wiggle them back and forth while gently pulling to dislodge their roots. Take care to support your basket by holding it firmly while carefully pulling on the stalks. Too much force can damage your basket! Wheatgrass is especially difficult to remove because its root systems are so massive. Plastic collanders are recommended in lieu of natural fiber baskets becuase of their ponderous roots.

Once out, you will notice the bottoms are full of root systems and hulls. You can cut the bottoms of the roots off or clean them. Cutting is faster and, for many, preferable. It is a personal preference. Place the sprouts in a basin of water, not too cold, but comfortable to the touch. Swish the sprouts and lift them out, leaving many of the hulls behind. Drain the cleaned sprouts in a colander (or basket) and pick any remaining hulls off by hand.

☞ ☞ *BASKET SPROUTERS CAN BE DAMAGED BY CARELESS HARVESTING OF WHEATGRASS, BUCKWHEAT & SUNFLOWER* ☜ ☜

As for *Wheatgrass*, there are no hulls. However, the bottom is full of seeds and roots. Wheatgrass is not a salad green. The blades are indigestible. Instead, the whole plant is juiced. Some people cut the ends of the hairy roots off and just juice the green blades. Others juice the roots, blades and all. Soil-free grown wheatgrass is mild tasting compared to the soil grown variety.

Buckwheat and sunflower are best harvested when at least 85% of the shells have fallen off. Choose the tallest sprouts and avoid the ones that have not yet developed their leaves; they are still growing. After the first harvest, store your basket of sprouts in the refrigerator where they will last another week. Take them out for a few hours each day if you want your sprouts to continue greening. Try to use purified water *(p. 134)* and organic seeds *(p. 65)*.

Getting the Shells Off

Buckwheat and sunflower have the largest leaves of any sprout in our sprouting seed repertoire and they are among the most popular and nutritious. But along with the large leaves comes large hulls or shells. How do you get these stubborn shells off? A few tips follow.

Moisture is essential. Moist shells loosen more readily than dry ones. Make sure you soak your sprouts thoroughly by immersing the whole basket in a sink full of water. Do not immerse until the roots have anchored themselves securely into the sprouter, which in the case of sunflower and buckwheat takes 4-6 days. Invert the basket and swish it back and forth watching the hulls fall out. Gently shake off the excess moisture and reposition your sprouter in the greenhouse tent. The greenhouse maintains the moisture level so the shells and tips of the sprouts are always moist.

Actual harvest day will vary according to temperature. Hot temperatures move things along faster. Harvest when at least 85% of the sprouts have surrendered their hulls. Stubborn hulls must be pulled off individually. That's life. It is still takes a lot less time and energy than outdoor gardening, pruning and weeding, or even standing in line at the supermarket. And, you get a powerful bonus--vitamins! Buckwheat is rich in manganese, choline, inositol and phospholipids. Sunflower is one of the richest protein sources of all leafy green sprouts--4% protein--and is also an excellent source of zinc.

How To Use Wheatgrass

Wheatgrass is used primarily as a healing juice, although small amounts can be taken in salad for fiber. Buckwheat is a delicate salad green like Bibb or Boston lettuce. Sunflower is hardy like spinach. You may eat or juice the whole sprout, including the roots and stems. Wheatgrass may be chewed to suck out the juice, but avoid swallowing the pulp as it is too fibrous. One to two ounces of wheatgrass juice per day is a valuable vitamin and mineral supplement. Larger amounts have many therapeutic benefits for which a special wheatgrass press is required. (For more about wheatgrass, read *Wheatgrass: Nature's Finest Medicine*, by this author.)

Cleaning and Maintenance

Cleaning and maintenance of the baskets that grow buckwheat and sunflower is similar to that of the smaller baskets but is more challenging. *(See cleaning sprouters p. 28.)* These roots are more massive and, as noted previously, the baskets can be destroyed if you yank the sprouts out carelessly. Follow these important steps for proper care.

1) When harvesting, pull out a few sprouts at a time so as to put as little strain as possible on the basket. Support the basket as you pull and be sure to take the sprouts out, roots and all. This leaves less for you to clean later.

2) Scoop off the leftover roots with a spatula or spoon. Plastic or wooden utensils, with their softer surfaces, are preferred because they are less likely to damage the natural fibers. Clean the basket using a vegetable or scrub brush. Do not try to clean out every root.

3) Allow baskets or collanders to dry thoroughly first by placing it in the sun or a warm oven. Then brush off the remaining rootlets with a dry brush. A small percentage of rootlets always remain behind but are of no consequence.

4) To sterilize your baskets, place them in boiling water for 3-5 minutes. You may also brighten them in a solution of ¼ cup Clorox per sink full of water for one plus hours. Increase concentration if necessary. Use hydrogen peroxide as an ecological alternative. *(See p. 53.)*

Mix 'em N' Match 'em

As an expert sprouter now, you may want to graduate to mixing several varieties in the same basket. This saves you space and effort and, once you have mastered the technique, can be easily done. The key is to mix only compatible varieties that mature at approximately the same time. Keep them within their same family and the sprouts will thrive happily. Here are some recommended mixes:

Alfalfa + Fenugreek + Red Clover

Alfalfa and red clover are cousins. They even look alike. Fenugreek, though not quite in the family, matures in 8 days while Alfalfa matures in 7 and Red Clover in 6. This means they will all be ready in about the same time. Five tablespoons (⅓ cup) makes about 1½ pounds of sprout lettuce. You can divide the seeds any way you wish. For example:

COMBO I		*CLUB II*		*GROUP III*	
2 Tbsp	Alfalfa	3 Tbsp	Alfalfa	3 Tbsp	Alfalfa
2 Tbsp	Clover	2 Tbsp	Clover	1 Tbsp	Fenugreek
1 Tbsp	Fenugreek	1 Tbsp	Clover		

Here comes the cabbage and mustard family...Watch out for these fellas--they're hot! Chinese cabbage, turnip, black mustard, kale, rapeseed, and radish are some of the members of this family and they are all easily mixed or matched. The smaller six inch diameter baskets are preferred for these boys because of their spicy personality-- a little lasts a long time.

Cabbage + Turnip + Mustard

These three look so much alike as seeds and as sprouts that you have to be an expert to tell them apart. The best test is to taste them. All are rather small sprouts less than an inch high. Mix them equally--one tablespoon each. Use no more than 3 tablespoons in the small (6 inch diameter) baskets. They will all peak in 5 days, but watch out for the warm weather. These boys have a germination rate of only 85-90% which means 10-15% of them will not sprout. Be careful, these few can cause your entire crop to go sour especially in hot weather. Remember to label your supplies so you can tell these seeds apart.

Kale and rapeseed are less common members of the cabbage family, but are delightful sprouters if you can find the seeds. They take 6-7 days to peak and mix well together or with their cabbage cousins.

Radish

Radish is the largest and heartiest member of this group. It is also more durable and easier to work with. It matures in 5 days, and matches nicely with any of the others. Because of its larger size (1½ inches or more), radish successfully bridges the genre gap and mixes nicely with alfalfa and red clover. Some good radish combinations are:

4 Radish Combo's

Ooh!   1 Tbsp Radish   *Ahh!*   1 Tbsp Radish
         4 Tbsp Alfalfa   3 Tbsp Alfalfa
         1 Tbsp Clover

Oh!   1 Tbsp Radish   *Wow!*   1 Tbsp Radish
         1 Tbsp Turnip   1 Tbsp Cabbage
         3 Tbsp Alfalfa   1 Tbsp Turnip

The fewer varieties you mix, the less chance for any problems. Mixing 2 or 3 varieties is recommended. Of course you can mix more, but make sure you are familiar with the different varieties and the percentage of germination of your particular lot before you mix too many at once.

Although mixing any of the above combinations will work well, another approach is to mate them side by side. Two varieties are easy to match, just divide your 5 tablespoons in half and lay your seeds down in two sides of your basket. Now watch two varieties grow side by side. Three varieties, although a little tricky, can be done by simply dividing your basket layout into three. It looks great!

Liquid Kelp

Nature's Finest Fertilizer

Is it possible for the most nutritious vegetables in the world to get even healthier? Yes, with soluble liquid kelp! Ordinarily, plants absorb minerals from soil. But in your soil-free kitchen garden, the only minerals they get come from the water. That is why it is so important to use quality water *(see water p. 134.)* If you can increase the nutrient level in that water, your sprouts will be healthier, grow bolder, store longer and have more nutrition to offer you.

Here's a short list of what you'll be adding to your sprouts: *Minerals* Calcium, magnesium, phosphorus, potassium, chromium, germanium, iodine, iron, manganese, molybdenum, strontium, vanadium, zinc; *Vitamins* A,B1,B2,C,D,E,K, carotene, pantothene, and the important vegetarian vitamin B-12; also 21 amino acids and *cell factors* such as auxins, giberellins, cytokinins, RNA, DNA, etc. *(See chart below.)* There are hundreds of different kinds of kelp, but choose the kind designed for plants and seedlings. It is very concentrated, but kelp will never "burn" your plants.

Sprouts normally have higher vitamin and mineral levels than regular vegetables because, as baby plants, their nutrients are more concentrated. But, with the addition of liquid kelp fertilizer, these levels are elevated to rival vegetables grown outdoors.

How To Use Liquid Kelp

1) **Soaking Stage.** It's simple. Just add a few drops of liquid kelp to your seeds during soaking. The soak water will take on the color of a dark tea and the seeds will absorb the nutrients.

2) **Misting.**   While the sprouts are growing, you may mist the seeds or leaves with your liquid kelp solution. *Misting with kelp is not a substitute for rinsing with plain water!* Always rinse your sprouts *first*. There is no limit to how many times you may apply the kelp mist. Mist your sprouts as much as twice per day for maximum nutrition or just once every two or three days. Plants have a remarkable ability to absorb nutrients through their leaves as well as their roots.

Mix enough liquid kelp with water to make the mixture look like a dark tea. Remove any sediment with a fine sieve before pouring into a mister gun or atomizer.

For House Plants, Too

Spray the kelp "tea" from your mister bottle onto your house plants' leaves and surfaces. The addition of a small amount of wetting agent or surfactant (such as liquid soap) prevents beading on the leaves. You may also add the tea directly to the soil once every 3 watering cycles.

Storage of Kelp

Your bottle of liquid Kelp is teeming with nutrients. But because it is stable, it can be stored on a cupboard shelf. If you live in a hot climate, store in a cool place.

Benefits

Kelp provides over 60 trace elements plus vitamins, amino acids (proteins), enzymes, alginates, polysachardies and cell growth factors that are normally found in soil. Some nutrients are actually more concentrated in kelp than in soil and are more available to the growing sprouts because they are readily assimilable. The nutrient boost the sprouts get actually makes them heartier and can improve taste and texture. During germination, the seeds multiply the vitamins and minerals they get from the kelp providing you with more minerals than if you drank the kelp liquid yourself.

Liquid kelp can be used for all plants, indoors or out, including trees, vines, ornamentals, vegetables and roots. It even assists compost piles by stimulating bacterial action. Because of its low nitrogen level, it will not burn. It should also be purged of the majority of its salt making it specifically suited for plants.

Analysis of Kelp Meal
Used to Make Liquid Kelp

Total Dry Matter	93.0%	Iron	600.0ppm
Soluble Organics	60.5%	Manganese	24.0ppm
Soluble Inorganics	32.5%	Zinc	33.0ppm
Nitrogen	00.87%	Bromine	0.6ppm
Phosphorous	00.14%	Cobalt	2.0ppm
Potassium	01.90%	Vanadium	0.7ppm
Calcium	11,900.ppm	Copper	0.5ppm
Chlorine	55,400.ppm	Chromium	0.5ppm
Magnesium	10,600.ppm	Germanium	0.1ppm
Sodium	19,400.ppm	Lead	0.4ppm
Sulphur	49,600.ppm	Molybdenum	0.6ppm
Aluminum	200.ppm	Nickel	5.0ppm
Boron	50.ppm	Silver	0.2ppm
Iodine	1,960.ppm	Strontium	0.4ppm

Plus...

Vitamin A	Vitamin D	21 Amino Acids
Vitamin B1	Vitamin E	Cytokinins
Vitamin B2	Vitamin F	Carotene
Vitamin B12	Niacin	Pantothene
Vitamin C	Choline	Auxins
		Giberellins

Sprouting Gelatinous Seeds

Chia, Cress, Psyllium, Flax

Gelatinous seeds are those which form a gel or slippery film upon soaking. The gel prohibits them from sprouting in jars or conventional plastic sprouters. Sprouters commonly used with these seeds are made of clay. However, they grow successfully in either the bag or basket method. They are very nutritious but require special instructions. Now, you can gain the benefit of these healthy seeds simply by using your basket sprouter.

Basket Integration Method

The most common gelatinous seeds are chia, flax, psyllium and cress. Many sprout devotees shun these seeds because they form a muscilaginous glue upon soaking. Gelatinous seeds are not the lepers of the sprout community and this rejection is outright sprout discrimination! The easiest way to enjoy these seeds is to integrate them with others such as alfalfa, cabbage, kale, turnip or red clover. Soak your seeds in the usual way, but substitute 1 tablespoon of gelatinous seed. For example, use 4 of alfalfa and 1 Tbsp. chia. Proceed to sprout as normal and enjoy. Here are some other successfully integrated combinations.

Mixing Gelatinous and Regular Seeds

Clan I		*Team II*		*Crew III*	
1 Tbsp	Psyllium	1 Tbsp	Chi	1 Tbsp	Chia
3 Tbsp	Alfalfa	2 Tbsp	Alfalfa	1 Tbsp	Kale
1 Tbsp	Cabbage	2 Tbsp	Clover	3 Tbsp	Clover

Mix your favorite selection in a medium size (8 inch) basket. Psyllium is mild in flavor, chia and cress are hot and flax is bitter. Of the entire group, flax and chia are the easiest to obtain and the easiest to sprout. Flax grows tall and looks great but only tastes good when the length of the shoot is equal to the length of the seed. Otherwise it is very bitter. The non-gelatinous seeds, alfalfa, etc. provide a bed for the gelatinous ones, so make sure that your gelatinous seeds make up only 15%-20% of the total seeds.

The Upside Down Method

A second method of growing these seeds requires a little more work but returns many aesthetic rewards. Soak 1-2 tablespoons of chia or other gelatinous seed for only 10 minutes. Using the small 6 inch basket, hold it upside down and spread the chia evenly all over the top and sides. Now get out your mister or atomizer and mist the chia thoroughly. Place the basket in the greenhouse tent leaving plenty of air. You do not need to tuck the bag under because you do not have a root system as with the traditional vertical method. Mist the chia once each day and the greens will start to show in one week. In 12 to 14 days the chia should be ½ to 1 inch long and ready for harvest. Chia is the most successful variety for this method. Just pull them out and enjoy.

Sprout Bag Method

Chia, flax, psyllium and cress cannot be sprouted using a jar, but they will sprout on top of a sprout bag. That's right, on top, not in the bag! Lay the bag out flat on a dish or a tray, then sprinkle a layer of flax, chia or other gelatinous seed, on top of the bag covering it fully but making sure they are only one level deep. Now, spray the seeds and bag heavily using a mister or atomizer (available in plant stores). Cover the bag loosely with plastic or insert it in one of your greenhouse tents or other covering to maintain moisture. The plastic prevents the seeds and the bag from drying out. This is crucial to the success of your crop, so take care to do this properly the first day and for the next 3 or 4 days. In approximately 10-14 days, your crop will be mature and stand ½ inch to 2 inches tall. Pluck carefully and use in salads. Store in a plastic bag in the refrigerator for up to a week. Experiment with the gelatinous seeds. Once you do, you are sure to stick to them!

Health Benefits Of Flax

Flax or linseed oil, our best source of vitamin F, has been an important health product for a long time, but now, it is becoming the latest rage. Dr. Max Gerson first recommended it for his cancer patients. Research in Germany, Austria and India confirms that linseed oil stimulates the immune system, inhibits the growth of cancer cells, and controls cholesterol and hypertension. Edible linseed oil is cold pressed from the flax seed. This wonderful plant not only gives us this special oil, but also linen, the raw material which is used to manufacture the *Flax Sprout Bag*--hence its name. The seed is also very healthful providing a mucilage which, like psyllium, helps cleanse the intestinal tract.

You can enjoy the benefits of this wonderful seed simply by blending ⅓ cup of flaxseed to a meal in a dry blender. Then add 1 cup of apple juice and 1 banana. Drink the mixture before it thickens. Follow it with more water or juice.

Other Sprouting Methods

The basket and sprout bag methods may be the most natural and the most aesthetically pleasing sprouters, but they are for household use and not commercial production.

The Colander Method

A basket, after all, is a colander, except that many colanders are made from plastic or aluminum. Although we have adjusted to the presence of plastic in our world, it is still an unsavory combination with food. However, it is part of American culture and omnipresent. Colanders are available in many sizes and if you require large amounts of sprouts, a large colander may be your best solution.

Make sure the seeds won't fall through the holes. If the holes are too large, grow the seeds for 1 to 2 days in the sprout bag first, then pour them into the colander for vertical growth.

About Aluminum Colanders

Many colanders are aluminum which is another unsavory food companion and also a very controversial one. Television commercials display it as if it is the kitchen's greatest gift. Health crusaders claim it to be a great poison. Still others say it will not hurt you unless you cook or use acids with it. You can decide for yourself, but, first, you should be able to identify aluminum products. Today's aluminum compounds are sometimes hard to differentiate from steel. You can determine if something is aluminum by making this simple test. Rub a tissue against an aluminum pot and look for a silvery shiny residue. This is aluminum oxide. Boil some water in an aluminum pot or just let water sit in it for a while. The longer the water sits the more you will see a whitish powder and pitting. These are aluminum oxides and other aluminum by-products. The more you heat aluminum the more it breaks down. Acids like lemon juice speed up the breakdown process. Ordinarily we do not notice these residues because they are absorbed into whatever food we are preparing.

Small, under-funded consumer safety organizations regularly do battle with the Food and Drug Administration over aluminum. But change is slow and frequently non-action is interpreted as sanctioning an unsafe product. Saccharine, red dye #2, nitrates, and DDT, all acknowledged poisons now, were accepted for a long time. At the very least, aluminum is a negative substance that many experts say draws the vitality out of food. Aluminum poisoning is now recognized as an insidious health enemy and doctors are starting to deal with it. Bamboo colanders, on the other hand, come from the fibers of a living plant. Which would you choose?

The Tray Method

Another vertical method uses a nylon or fiberglass screen tucked inside a rectangular dish or tray. The screen serves as a footing for the sprouts to root in, with the tray as the base. Again our first concern is a question of materials. Though nylon and fiberglass are not serious health threats, they are not as preferable as natural fibers. The nylon screen becomes embedded with sprouts and is very difficult to clean especially on a daily basis. With these small reservations aside, this is an excellent method for growing sprouts in quantity.

Obtain standard seedling trays, 11 inches by 22 inches, from your local nursery and garden center store. These trays come with or without holes. You may choose either with some caveats.

With Holes. If you choose these, you must first pre-sprout the seeds for 1 to 2 days in a sprout bag. Pour the started seedlings into the tray and spread the seeds evenly with a hose or dish sprayer. Some seedlings will fall through the holes so expect a small amount of loss. As the mat of roots develops, less and less will be lost. Angle these trays for a few minutes to drain excess water. The presence of holes is deceiving. They do not drain the trays completely.

Without Holes. Choose this tray if you cannot afford to have any water leakage in your growing location. It is not a waterproof solution, however, because the tray is usually wet from watering and would need to be towel dried if you cannot tolerate any wetness on the bottom. This type of tray requires careful drainage. As with the perforated trays, hold them at an angle and wait for the water to drain off. The draining process is more difficult than draining a basket sprouter, but the trade off is higher volume and easy cleaning.

Greenhouses are again necessary with the tray method, but some seedling trays can be purchased with pre-fab clear plastic greenhouses that fit snugly on the top. Many of these pre-fab greenhouse seedling trays also contain insert cups for soil growing. These inserts are not useful for sprouting so put them aside or recycle. Harvesting and cleaning the sprouts is easier in this method than the basket sprouter because the inside surface is solid and does not provide a means for the plant to root. To harvest, simply remove the sprouts. Clean the bottoms which contain many fallen hulls by immersing and swishing them in a basin of water. This is one small disadvantage. The sprouts cannot be inverted for convenient hull cleaning as in the basket method. However, there are no weaves here to clean. Simply rinse the plastic bottom clean with a hose or sterilize it with boiling water or hydrogen peroxide. The tray method is a convenient way to produce a 3 pound yield per tray from 1 cup of seeds. Follow the same seed varieties, harvest times and rinsing practices as described for the basket sprouting method.

Commercial Sprouters

Commercial sprout farmers have different considerations than the home indoor gardener. They must minimize growing times, maximize volume, decrease costs including labor, streamline by eliminating varieties that increase labor or fall below sales levels and first and foremost produce only what produces profits. If you are thinking of starting a commercial sprout business because you like sprouts, consider that it requires large investment in equipment, warehouse, staff and takes marketing expertise. Plan your business carefully before starting. Although you may love sprouts, you should take the whole picture into consideration. You may very well end up with your hands in ledgers more than the sprouts. Commercial sprout farming equipment rinses sprouts hundreds of times per day to increase rate of growth. For more information about purchasing commercial equipment, $5,000 and up, and starting your own commercial sprout farming business, contact the industry's trade organization, the International Sprout Growers Association. *(See Resources, p. 181.)*

Automatic Sprouters

The word "automatic" is very exciting. Let's face it, we Americans want it fast and we want it easy. Unless of course we're gardeners. Isn't automation the antithesis of gardening? A sprout bag is certainly not automatic, but it's fast. It involves less time and labor to sow, harvest and clean than automatic machines that cost 300 times its price. Do you need an automatic sprouter? If you are new to sprouting and can't decide, here's what to consider.

Volume: if you have a sprout growing business, are a volume home sprouter, or grow wheatgrass in the quantities usually required for therapy, automatic machines become a necessity. *Price:* while most home sprouters cost between $15 and $25, automatic sprouters can cost between $200 and $1,200. *Time and labor:* How much work will an automatic sprouter save you? They save the daily job of rinsing, but not all automatic sprouters are created equal. Many machines still require certain tasks such as the soaking and sowing of the seeds and harvesting and cleaning of the equipment. Some require you to refill the water tank daily. *Space:* These machines take up more space than regular home sprouters. *Hook Up:* Many machines, but not all, require electricity & plumbing connections. Evaluate the ease and expense of the installation. *Quality:* Evaluate the quality and features of the device and the company behind it. *Reality:* All automatic sprouters involve some work such as sowing seeds, harvesting sprouts and cleaning equipment. Unfortunately, the only way to enjoy sprouts without any work is to   buy them at the store.

Wheatgrass growing in a popular automatic (electric) sprouter. Water from the bottom reservoir rises up and sprinkles the sprouts growing on top. This sprouter is technically semi-automatic. The user pours in the water once every one-two days. But, there is no plumbing is required. *(See Resources p. 181.)*

Questions & Answers

With

Sproutman

DEAR SPROUTMAN: My sprouts are brown, small, and all dry on top. They have never grown up even though I've waited the proper number of days.   *--M. P. Chent*

DEAR MR. CHENT: Your sprouts are suffering from a condition known as "oishgetrichundosis." This means they are all dried up. They were probably not protected well enough with the greenhouse tent during the first few days. Once dried up, sprouts will not grow, even if you treat them properly later.

DEAR SPROUTMAN: There is a white, furry-like mold on top of my basket sprouts. What happened?   *--Mr. White*

DEAR MR. WHITE: You went away for the weekend and forgot to take your sprouts! Sprouts do not like to be ignored. Mold will develop if you skip one or two rinsings. Don't skip out on your sprouts. Rinse thoroughly by showering or immersing them in water. Do not use a mister. Throw these sprouts away, and donate the mold to your nearest hospital.

DEAR SPROUTMAN: My sprouts smell like ammonia. What happened?   *--Mr. Clean*

DEAR MR. CLEAN: First of all, never rinse your sprouts with ammonia. Ammonia, NH_3, is a nitrogen compound derived from the decomposition of protein. If you smell ammonia, it is proof that your sprouts are rich in protein, but it is also the first sign of rot. Do not eat these sprouts even if they look good. They will become limp and soggy soon. Sometimes a thorough bath will help, but if the smell persists, send them to the nearest compost and start again.

There are 4 reasons why your sprouts may have decomposed.

1)   They suffocated from too little air in the greenhouse tent.
2)   They suffered from sunstroke or heat exhaustion.
3)   They were not cleaned well enough and the hulls started to decay.
4)   They were stored longer than their life expectancy and expired from natural causes.

DEAR SPROUTMAN: It has been a week, and my alfalfa still is not green. What have I done wrong?   *--Mr. Green*

DEAR MR. GREEN: These sprouts are suffering from lack of light and lack of warmth. If your home is very cold, you can warm your sprouts by rinsing them in lukewarm water. Test the water first to make sure it is not hot. If your apartment is dark, invest in some Vita-Lites. They will do the best job. Regular incandescent bulbs or grow lights will work, but be careful they do not create too much heat for your sprouts.

DEAR SPROUTMAN: My sprouts need more greening, but I am afraid to take them out of the refrigerator because the weather is so hot.   *--Mr. F. Raide*

DEAR MR. RAIDE: Keep them refrigerated during the day, but give them Vita-Lite at night. Temperatures are cooler at night, so you can risk taking them out. Vita-Lites, unlike incandescent bulbs, generate little or no heat and provide a full spectrum of light.

DEAR SPROUTMAN: It has been about 5 days after my first harvest. But I still have more than I can possibly eat in the next few days. *--Mr. X. Esse*

DEAR MR. ESSE: Give your sprouts a good cleaning and refrigerate them to extend their life.

DEAR SPROUTMAN: It is now 7 days after planting. I have just had my first harvest. The weather is very hot and the sprouts look limp and soggy in spots. *--V. Rehut*

DEAR MR. REHUT: These sprouts are suffering from heatstroke. Clean them thoroughly, throwing out any rotted portions. Refrigerate and finish as soon as possible.

DEAR SPROUTMAN: I've got a furry white growth on the roots of my radish sprouts. Is that mold? *--I. Whiree.*

DEAR MR. WHIREE: Don't worry. It is not mold...yet. The "white fur" on the radish is actually cilia hairs that the young rootlets throw off to seek water. It indicates that the sprouts need more forceful rinsing. If the situation continues, mold will indeed develop. When you see a *gray* colored fur with black spots, it is genuine mold and should not be eaten.

DEAR SPROUTMAN: I've noticed some of my baskets are darkening. Is that mold? *--Dr. Gray.*

DEAR DR. GRAY: Dark seeds like sunflower, garlic and buckwheat dissolve the dye of their shells from repeated watering. This is not mold, but the large fallen shells from these seeds can decay. At first sign of graying or spotting, wash and brush the area with water. After you've harvested your sprouts, you may choose to bleach your baskets clean with food grade 35% potency hydrogen peroxide or bleach.

DEAR SPROUTMAN: How do you get the shells off these sunflowers. They're a twisted mess!   *--Dejected*

DEAR DEJECTED: Take care to let your sunflower roots anchor into the basket during the first 5 days of growth. This enables them to grow upright. Use plenty of water pressure, but don't dislodge them from rooting. With normal vertical growth, the shells will fall off automatically.

DEAR SPROUTMAN: I like your sprouting method, but must I use the greenhouse tent?   *--Discontent*

DEAR DISCONTENT: Yes, the greenhouse maintains moisture and temperature. Without it, the sprouts dry out and decay. If you prefer, you can make your own greenhouse by constructing a frame box with plastic walls. Or you may purchase a rigid greenhouse box. *(See Resources.)*

DEAR SPROUTMAN: I'm growing your Kale sprouts and have noticed that they are so tightly packed in the basket that it is tough to pull them out. Why is this so?   *--Ty Fisted*

DEAR TY: Kale, mustard and turnip are rather short sprouts 1/2--1 inch in length. Because they are so small, they can easily get packed in tightly leaving little room to grab. The solution is twofold. First, use less seed, approximately 2 tablespoons per 6 inch sprouter. Second, involves a technique of partially disturbing the seeds during the rooting phase. The rooting phase is the stage of growth about the third or fourth day when the roots seek to anchor into the weave of the baskets. Ordinarily, one washes the seeds with fervor the first and second day, disturbing their orientation without worry. After that, you usually let them anchor undisturbed. A well anchored sprout grows straight up, stands tall and can be bathed in the inverted position once mature. But for these tight fisted seeds, a little disruption makes the harvest process easier. So, loosen up!

DEAR SPROUTMAN: My clover is not growing so well. I bought the in August and it worked fine. Now, 6 months later, the sprouts are much smaller. I sprout them in the same spot on the windowsill and I store the seed in a jar with a rubber sealed cap and keep them cool. Have they gone bad?
--Ed Grover

DEAR ED: The fact that the seed grows at all means it is viable. Both clover and its cousin alfalfa can endure in storage for many years with little effect on germination. The difference you are seeing is not because of the seed, but the season. Unless you live in the sub-tropics, January sprouting is a lot slower than August. Clover should mature in 6 days in August. But in order for them to grow big and tall, you may have to wait 9 days in January, especially if you grow them near the window where it is cold. When you rinse your growing basket sprouts, use luke warm water. The rinse water should never be hot to the touch, but warmer water warms up the cold seeds and helps speed up the growing process.

DEAR SPROUTMAN: My friend tells me that you can't grow sprouts in Florida because the heat and humidity cause too much mold. So, although I like your sprout bag and bamboo sprouters very much, I am sticking to the jar method because I know glass is resistant to mold.   *--Carl Molden*

DEAR CARL: Florida isn't the only place that is hot and humid. As a matter of fact, where I live in the Northeast, the summers get very hot and humid. Not only that, every greenhouse I have ever been in is hot and humid. My point is that Florida, by virtue of its humidity, does not make it impossible to grow sprouts. It is true that some varieties cannot tolerate the heat as well as others, but rest assured, you can grow sprouts successfully in Florida, all it takes is a little extra rinsing. First of all, stop using the jar. Most jars provide too small an enclosed space for the sprouts and heat builds up dramatically. Unlike a sprout bag or bamboo sprouter, there are few air holes in a jar for the sprouts to breath. You can probably cook sprouts in a jar on a hot day! Washing is everything. When it is hot, rinse 3 times per day. Always, use cold water. It is the rinse water that cools the sprouts. The only temperature that matters is the one inside the sprouter, not in your house. Put your hand in and feel it. If it's hot, rinse more often. Make sure the plastic greenhouse bag is propped up like a tent so there is plenty of air to circulate. The more air, the cooler the sprouts. Mold is induced in low air environments. Remember to refrigerate your crop as soon as it is mature.

DEAR SPROUTMAN: I have one of the water filters you recommend. I dip my sprout bags in a basin of this pure water and they turn out just fine. But your instructions for rinsing the basket sprouters request that they be "showered" and "flushed" with water. How do you do this with a water filter that does not allow for a spray attachment?   *--Unattached*

DEAR UNATTACHED: Perhaps a dating service can help. But as far as your water filter goes, here is the connection. Obtain a watering can with a shower-head nozzle. Fill the can with pure water. Water your sprouting baskets by holding the can aloft and letting the pure water shower down. Sprouts that are 1-3 days old require only about 5 seconds of rinsing. As the sprouts get bigger, there are more of them and they should be rinsed for approximately 10 seconds. Holding your watering can aloft increases the force at which the water hits the sprouts. It is actually this water pressure that *flushes* away mold and other bacteria preventing their development. Both sufficient water pressure and contact time are necessary to maintain a healthy, mold-free crop.

DEAR SPROUTMAN: I want to stock up on seeds, but how long will these things last?   *--N. Dure*

DEAR MR. DURE: Vegetable seeds such as alfalfa, and beans such as mung, can store for years. Germination will remain high, if kept cool and dry. A basement or other cool spot is ideal. Most seeds store happily at a modest 60 degree F. temperature. But be aware, most cellars are also wet. Make sure you use a moisture-proof container. Glass and plastic are both okay. Use colored glass if possible or throw a cloth over the jar to keep out light. Paper and plastic bags are not desirable for storage beyond the short term.

DEAR SPROUTMAN: You said I could sprout year-round. So I did. But my wheat, sunflowers and millet are literally flying around the house in the form of moths. What are you going to do about it! *--I.M. Bugged*

DEAR MR. BUGGED: Cool down. Cold and prevention are your salvation. Grains and sunflower seeds have a more limited storage life than vegetable seeds and are susceptible to internal bug development in the hot summer. Cold is the solution. Refrigerate small quantities or otherwise keep them cool during the summer. If you have grain bugs and moths, freeze the seed to destroy the bugs and sterilize their larvae. Bugs are like pollution. They are much easier to prevent than to clean up. Most of the grains will store bug-free for years if kept at an ideal temperature of 40°F.-50°F. Freezing the grains is also acceptable in most cases. Constant temperature is important because wide temperature fluctuations reduce the germination rate. If you are unable to keep them this cold, and your storage temperatures range 60°F and above, I recommend using a form of diatomaceous earth. This natural silica product is mined from dried lakes. The clay-like powder is wiped onto surfaces of the storage container and kills the moths by dehydration.

DEAR SPROUTMAN: My mother wants to know if you make
house calls?   *--Dearest Daughter*

DEAREST DAUGHTER: Neither wind, nor rain, nor sleet, nor
snow, nor dark of night will keep Sproutman from a needy
sprout. Prepare the Sproutmobile. *Sproutman's* Coming To Dinner!

REVIEW

Using A Vertical Sprouter

What Seeds to Sprout

Alfalfa	Clover	Fenugreek	Garlic
Radish	Mustard	Cabbage	Onion
Pea Greens	Turnip	Psyllium	Chia
Buckwheat	Wheatgrass	Sunflower	Kale

Soak & Drain

Soak 3 to 5 tablespoons of seed in an 8 oz jar of pure water. The hot seeds (radish, cabbage, mustard, turnip, kale) are best in the smaller baskets using 3 Tbsp. amounts. Alfalfa, fenugreek, and clover are best with 4 to 5 Tbsp. in the larger baskets. After approximately 6-8 hours of soaking, pour the seeds into the basket and let drain. Keep at an angle for about 3 minutes or until the dripping has stopped. Whenever possible use organic seeds and purified water.

Rinsing

Rinse at least twice a day with cold water. Use a shower or shower adapter on your faucet. Sprouts prefer this to the hard force of a faucet. Spraying or misting is not enough. Hint: good, thorough rinsing and draining avoids most problems.

The Greenhouse

House the basket in the greenhouse tent. Create a large bubble of air in the plastic to ensure adequate air circulation. Your greenhouse should look like a tent or a dome. Tuck the open end of the bag under the basket. It does not have to be air tight. The basket remains in the greenhouse tent at all times except for rinsing. It retains moisture, maintains temperature, and allows light to penetrate.

Light

Darkness is not necessary, but keep the basket away from strong light for the first 3 or 4 days. Then move to a bright area but always avoid the heat from direct sunlight. If you do not have natural light, use Vita-lites or grow lamps.

Harvesting

Most varieties will be ready for harvest in 5-8 days. When ready, they will appear fully green. Harvest by plucking from the surface so as to allow the younger sprouts to keep on growing.

Storage

After the first harvest, refrigerate your baskets and, depending on the variety, they will generally last another week. Take them out for a few hours each day allowing them to continue to green.

Cleaning

After the fourth or fifth day, you may immerse the whole

basket in a basin of water, even turning it upside down! Make sure your roots have anchored themselves to the basket before trying this. Agitate the basket and watch how easily the hulls fall out. This permits washing and rinsing at the same time.

Yield

Five tablespoons of alfalfa yield up to two pounds of sprouts. And each basket keeps on producing for three or more generations from only one batch of seed. Because of the large surface exposed to light and the vertical direction of their growth, your vertical sprouter yields a greater number of mature, clean sprouts with a higher nutritional value and more chlorophyll than sprouts grown in a jar.

REVIEW
The Sprout Bag

1) Place 1-2 cups of your favorite grains or beans in a jar and soak in pure water for 12 hours.

2) Pour the soaked beans into the sprout bag and hang on a hook or lay in dish rack to drain. Immerse the whole bag in pure water twice daily.

3) Bean and grain sprouts mature in 3-5 days. Keep them refrigerated after that for a week or more and rinse every second day.

SPROUTMAN'S SPROUT CHART

Variety	Tbsp	# Days	Method	Skill	Taste	USE
Alfalfa	4-5	7	Tray	Beg.	Mild, all purpose	Salad, Juice
Lentil	1 cup	4-5	Bag/Jar	Beg.	Crisp, crunchy	Salad, Steamed veg.
Fenugreek	4-5	7-8	Tray	Beg.	Piquant, tall	Salad, Relish
Mung	1 cup	4-5	Bag/Jar	Med.	Crisp, crunchy	Salad, Steamed veg.
Onion	2-3	12	Tray	Adv.	Very onion	Salad, Spice
Cabbage	2-3	5-6	Tray	Med.	Strong cabbage	Salad, Juice, Relish
Wheatgrass	1 cup	10-14	Tray/soil	Adv.	Strong	Juice, Therapy
Soybean	2 cup	4	Bag	Adv.	Big, hard	Cooking, casseroles
Buckwheat	5	10	Tray	Adv.	Delicate, big	Salad, Juice
Garlic	2-3	12	Tray	Adv.	Powerful garlic	Salad, Juice, Spice
Kamut	2 cup	3-4	Bag/Jar	Beg.	Hearty, crunchy	Wheatgrass, Breads
Radish	2-3	5-6	Tray	Beg.	Robust radish	Salad, Juice
Adzuki	1 cup	4-5	Bag/Jar	Med.	Crisp, crunchy	Salad, Steamed veg.
Sunflower	5-6	9-10	Tray	Med.	Hearty, big	Salad, Juice
Green Pea	1+cup	4-5	Bag/Jar	Beg.	Hearty, big	Steamed veg.
Hard Wheat	2 cup	2-3	Bag/Jar	Beg.	Sweet crunchy	Bread, snack
Chia	3–5	12	Basket	Adv.	Mild, gelatinous	Snack, treat
Garbanzo	2 cup	4	Bag/Jar	Adv.	Hummus taste	Dips & spreads
Broccoli	2-3	5-6	Tray	Med.	Gusty broccoli	Salad, juice, therapy
Grey Sunflowr	1 cup	2	Bag/Jar	Med.	Nutty	Snack, salad, spread
Peanut	2 cup	7	Bag	Adv.	Big, gusty	Dry roasted snack
Soft Wheat	2 cup	2-3	Bag/Jar	Beg.	Sweet, crunchy	Cookies, rejuvelac
Clover	4-5	6-7	Tray	Beg.	Spicier alfalfa	Salad
Spelt	1 cup	3	Bag/Jar	Beg.	Crunchy	Sprout bread
Brown Mustard	2-3	5-6	Tray	Med.	Hot, tiny	Spice
Pea Lettuce	5-6	8-9	Tray	Med.	Mild, crisp, big	Salad
Quinoa	1 cup	3	Bag/Jar	Beg.	Crunchy	Grain or salad
Rye	1 cup	3	Bag/Jar	Beg.	Crunchy	Sprout bread

The Sprout Oath

For Best Results Recite Each Day

I WILL . . .

STAND UP STRAIGHT AND TALL
ALWAYS FOLLOW THE SUN
THINK GREEN THOUGHTS
DRINK PLENTY OF WATER
BATHE AT LEAST TWICE A DAY
LISTEN TO CLASSICAL MUSIC
KEEP MY HEAD HIGH
STICK TO MY ROOTS
GO TO BED AT DUSK
SERVE AND BE SERVED
BE SPROUTFUL AND MULTIPLY

A GOOD SPROUT IS . . .

Loyal
  Friendly
    Courteous
      Kind
        Trustworthy
          Obedient
            Helpful
              Clean
                Brave

Be Good To Your Sprouts
And They Will Be True To You!

Sprout

IDENTIFICATION

MISSION

DEAR READER:

As you may know, the Food and Drug Administration (FDA) has occasionally investigated non-traditional foods and obstructed their passage through interstate commerce. In the past, everything from vitamins to apricot pits has been pulled off natural food store shelves. Now, through a secret memo intercepted by Sproutman, *we discover they are going after sprouts. What follows is the contents of a memo from the Federal Bureau of Investigation (FBI) to the F.D.A. identifying various sprout "suspects" which we provide to you for your edification.*

Officer: Okay men, this assignment is code named *G.S.I.D.* -- *Green Sprout Identification* mission. Your job, should you decide to accept it, is to search out all sprouts of every size, color and shape. And when you find them...eat 'em! Any questions? Okay, here's what to look for...

Radish: He's a fair-sized fellow, gotta big head with a notch in it. Very colorful this guy, usually seen with a red back, a green head, and a white tail. Watch him, he's hot!

Cabbage: This guy's a friend of the radish and frequently hangs out with him. A little guy with a light green complexion, parts his hair in the middle, and has a white tail. Sometimes speaks in Chinese.

Turnip: This guy's a relative of the cabbage, but is a little taller and has a tinge of red on the back of his neck. Hangs out with the cabbage, but is sharper, so watch him!

Black Mustard: One of the meanest of them all. He's rough. You'll find that he's real tight-fisted and a tough guy to uproot. Looks like the cabbage-same size, same notch in the head, but with a darker complexion. Don't get too close, or he'll burn ya!

Alfalfa: Shrewd. Been around a long time, has deep roots, and connections with the Arabs. He's tall and thin, long white legs, dark green face and a smooth oval head. He's strong.

Red Clover: A cousin of alfalfa, slightly smaller with a lighter complexion. He's got a fat head, but that same smooth face. Hard to tell 'em apart. He can bite!

Red Pea: A slick and slivery lass that towers over other greenery like a Giraffe peering over a herd of sheep. Though she's long and slender and sports a large green umbrella, she's a bit tough and a lot to chew on.

Fenugreek: Big guy. Biggest of the lot. Taller than the alfalfa and he's got more body to him. Has a smooth oval face with a deep emerald green color. Looks innocent, but after you got him locked him in your jaw, he'll surprise ya.

Buckwheat: Very classy lady. Poses as a wheat when she's really not. Nice long white legs with a light green color. Looks like a four leaf clover, but is only two. Very mild face with succulent lips. Stays on land only. Watch her. She's a temptress that can lure the best of you.

Sunflower: This guy's a monster! There ain't nothin' bigger than him. What a body, big, strong, but has light colored legs. You can almost mistake him for a white guy. Huge dark green biceps. The older ones have a hairy beard. Stays on land. Watch this guy. He's got muscles you ain't never even heard of. His one weakness--needs to drink a lot of water.

Broccoli: All right fella's, we're at the end of the list and this may be your hardest. Why? Because he's got a lot of protection around him—a lot of very powerful little friends called 'enzymes.' Keeps trouble out. But he's small, see. A little green guy. A cousin of the cabbage with same small, green looks but watch out—he's got a bite to him.

Okay troopers, you have your orders. I know this is a tough assignment so if anyone wants to back out now, just step forward. And to show ya there's no hard feelings, I'm gonna treat you to a nice meal—how's a juicy red steak sound to ya? The rest of you, no eating till you find your sprout!

The sprouts are all hiding out in the sprout house. In order to pick 'em out, we've got to know what they look like. That's why we call this S.I.D.M.—Sprout Identification Mission.

RESOURCES

Sprouting Seeds and Supplies

Seeds in Natural Food Stores. Packaged seeds are superior to bulk seeds because the latter lose germination from exposure to the elements. Better still are brands that specify their devotion to sprouting and include a germination count on the label. If you see a packaged seed that is not on *Sproutman's Sprout Chart* or the chart in this book, it may not be reliable for sprouting. The author tests a full line of sprouting seeds which is available in many health food stores and via mail order through the *Healthy Eating Catalog* (below).

Healthy Eating Catalog. Summertown, TN. 800-695-2241, fax 931-964-2291. Full line of *Sproutman* tested organic sprouting seeds, sprouters, and other organic foods. Also sells the *Freshlife Automatic Sprouter* (p.164) . www.Healthy-Eating.com

The Sprout House. East Meredith, NY. 800-777-6881. Full line of organic sprouting seeds. Originally founded by Sproutman in 1980. Now Rita owns and delivers great service. www.SproutHouse.com

Johnny's Selected Seeds. Winslow, ME. 207-861-3900, fax 800-437-4290. Organic sprouting seeds from this distinguished organic vegetable seed catalog. www.Johnnyseeds.com

Organic Provisions. Richboro, PA. 800-490-0044, fax 215-443-7087. www.OrgFood.com Internet supplier of organic sprouting seeds and natural foods. Wholesale and retail.

Sproutpeople. Gay Mills, WI. 608-735-4735, fax 608-735-4736.
Organic seeds. Ask for Gil. www.sproutpeople.com

Garden Spots Finest. New Holland, PA. 800-829-5100,
717-354-4936. Wholesale and retail of natural foods including organic sprouting seeds. www.gardenspotsfinest.com

Walton Feed. P.O. Box 307, Montpelier, ID 83254. Emergency
food supplies and sprouting seeds. www.waltonfeed.com

Sproutable Quinoa. White Mountain Farm. Ernie New, 8890 Lane 4
North, Mosca, CO 81146. 800-364-3019, fax 719-378-2897.

Manufacturers

Seed & Grain Technologies. Las Vegas, NV. 702-869-4662, 9-2pm
PST. Multi-level automatic sprouters and wheatgrass growers for
home and professional use. www.easygreen.com

International Specialty Supply (ISS). Cookeville, TN. 800-277-
7688. fax 615-526-8338. Manufacturer and supplier to commercial
sprout companies of large scale sprout farming equipment. Also line
of mostly non-organic sprouting seeds. www.Sproutnet.com

Hydroponics: Canada's Office of Urban Agriculture. Vancouver BC
Canada. 604-685-5832, fax 604-685-0431. Promotes growing food in
cities. Info on sprouting, rooftop gardens, composting toilets, horti-
culture therapy, and community gardens. www.cityfarmer.org

Clinics, Teaching Centers, Associations

Hippocrates Health Institute. 1443 Palmdale Court, West Palm
Beach, FL 33411. 800-842-2125. 561-471-8876. Full wheatgrass
training, sprout growing and live-in health program. Includes raw
foods and sprouts cuisine. www.hippocratesinst.com

Ann Wigmore Foundation. PO Box 399, San Fidel NM 87049.
505-552-0595. Ann Wigmore was the originator of wheatgrass therapy, buckwheat and sunflower greens. This is a new raw foods

therapy and retreat center. www.wigmore.org
LiveFood@Wigmore.org

Ann Wigmore Institute. PO Box 429, Rincon, PR 00743.
787-868-6307, fax 868-2430. Active retreat center in Puerto Rico on
the beach. Full training and live-in program following Ann Wigmore's
wheatgrass and live foods therapy. www.AnnWigmore.org

Optimum Health Institute. San Diego, CA. 800-993-4325.
619-464-3346. One of the original wheatgrass and raw foods training
centers, inspired by Ann Wigmore. Full training and live-in program
in wheatgrass and live foods therapy. Wheatgrass juicers and organic
sprouting seeds. www.OptimumHealth.org

Optimum Health Institute - Austin, Texas 800-993-4325 for reservations. 512-303-4817. Cedar Creek, TX. Smaller but newer version of
the San Diego center above. www.OptimumHealth.org

Tree of Life. Gabriel Cousins, MD. PO Box 1080, Patagonia, AZ
85624. 520-394-2520. Spiritual, eco-retreat center with organic Ko-
sher livefood cuisine, plenty of sprouts and wheatgrass. Includes private consultations with this renowned medical doctor and author.
Juice fasting retreats. www.treeoflife.nu

Hippocrates Health Centre Of Australia. Elaine Ave, Mudgeeraba
Gold Coast, Queensland 4213 Australia, for brochure. Tel (07)
5530-2860. Ann Wigmore inspired live-in training program for fasting, wheatgrass, juices and raw foods. www.hippocrates.com.au

Cancer Control Society. Los Angeles, CA. 323-663-7801. Organization that helps cancer patients find alternative and non-traditional
cancer therapies. Bus trips to Mexican clinics. Seminars, referrals,
annual convention. www.cancercontrolsociety.com

Foundation for Advancement in Cancer Therapies (FACT). PO Box
1242, Old Chelsea Station, New York, NY 10113. 212-741-2790. Fax
212-924-3634. Organization that helps cancer patients find alternative and non-traditional cancer therapies. Seminars, referrals, annual convention.

Center for Advancement in Cancer Education. 300 E Lancaster #100, Wynnewood, PA 19096. 610-642-4810. Educational organization helping cancer victims find successful, non-traditional therapies. Seminars, annual convention. www.BeatCancer.org

International Sprout Growers Association (ISGA), Seattle, WA. 800-572-3015. Commercial sprout and grass growers trade association. A must for professional growers. www.ISGA-Sprouts.org

General

Rhio's Raw Energy Hotline. 212-343-1152. A raw/live foods resource directory announcing classes and events in the New York metro area. Ask for Rhio new raw foods cookbook. Visit: www.RawFoodInfo.com

San Francisco Live Food Enthusiasts. The Sproutline 415-751-2806. San Francisco, CA. Telephone listing of live foods pot-lucks, lectures and outings in the San Francisco area.

RawTimes. An excellent website resource for testimonials, email forums, recipes, restaurant reviews, networking, events and book reviews on living foods diet. www.rawtimes.com

Loreta's Living Foods. Consultations on living foods and wheatgrass by this experienced teacher who worked with Dr. Ann Wigmore. 610-648-0241, fax 610-722-0680. lvainius@aol.com

Viktoras Kulvinskas. Pioneer in wheatgrass, raw foods and sprouts, offers consultations. email: youthing@alltel.net

Sproutman. The author gives private consultations on a variety of health and diet topics. 413-528- 5200. Fax 413-528-5201. Sproutman@Sproutman.com   www.Sproutman.com

Related Products

Gourmet Greens. 802-875-3820, ext.4. Chester, VT. Nationwide next day delivery of organic wheatgrass, radish, sunflower and pea shoots. Wheatgrass juicers. www.GourmetGreens.com

Food Grade Hydrogen Peroxide in non-hazardous 6% concentrated form but made from original 35% concentrate. Contact: *The Family News.* 800-284-6261. 305-759-9500. Miami Shores, FL. www.familyhealthnews.com

Other Books

The Sprout Garden by Mark Braunstein. Includes sprouting information and recipes. $12.95. ISBN#1-57067-073-0. 800-695-2241.

Living in the Raw. Recipes for a Healthy Lifestyle by Rose Lee Calabro. 800-695-2241. www.Healthy-Eating.com

Survival Into the 21st Century and *Sprout for the Love of Every Body.* both by sprouts and wheatgrass pioneer Rev. Viktoras Kulvinskas, MS. 800-593-2665, 515-472-5105.

Warming Up to Living Foods by Elysa Markowitz. $15.95. Raw foods, vegan recipes. 888-254-7336. www.greenpower.com

BIBLIOGRAPHY

[1]   Ames, Bruce N. "Dietary Carcinogens and Anti-carcinogens"
        Science Vol. 221. September 23, 1983

[2]   Kulvinskas, Victoras, *Survival Into The 21st Century* 21st
        Century Publications, Fairfield, Iowa.

[3]   Kulvinskas, Victoras, *Nutritional Evaluation of Sprouts and
        Grasses* 21st Century Publications, Fairfield, Iowa. 1978.

[4]   Bland, Jeffrey, Ph.D, Berquist, Barbara. "Nutrient Content Of
        Germinated Seeds." *Journal of the John Bastyr College of
        Naturopathic Medicine.* Vol 2 No 1, June 1980.

[5]   Heritage, Ford. *Composition and Facts About Food.* Health
        Research Press. Mokelumne Hill, CA. 1968.

[6]   Medallion Laboratories report #88011589 10/24/88 for Mon-
        tana Flour & Grain PO Box 808, Big Sandy, MT 59520.

[7]   Quinoa Corporation of America PO Box 1039, Torrance, CA
        90505. Plus USDA nutritional content of foods.

[8]   Recetas a Base De Quinoa. Ministry of Agriculture, Inter-
        American Grain Producers. 1953.

[9]   Dr. Paul Talalay, Johns Hopkins Medical School, Baltimore,
        MD. *The Proceedings of the National Academy of Sciences.*
        Also, Dr. Lee Wattenberg, University of Minnesota in Minne-
        apolis, a pioneer in the field of identifying anti-Cancer chemi-
        cals in food.

[10]   International Sprout Growers Assoc. 7946 Pocket Road #18
        Sacramento, CA 95831.

[11]   *Bio-Dynamic Literature*, Box 253 Wyoming, RI 02898. Alan
        Ismond, Simplot Aquaculture, 20875 Wagner Road, Caldwell,
        ID 83605.

[12]   Richard L. Sauer, Johnson Space Center; W. Scheld and J.W.
        Magnuson of PhytoResource Reseach Inc. *NASA Tech Briefs*,
        June 1989.

[13]   Malinow, M.R; Bardana, E.J. Jr; Pirofsky, B: Craig, S.; McLaugh-
        lin, P.; *Science* April 23, 1982, p415-7. ISSN 0036-8075. Sys-
        temic lupus erythematosus-like syndrome in monkeys fed
        alfalfa sprouts: role of a nonprotein amino acid.

[14]   Montanaro, A.; Bardana, E.J. Jr. Dietary amino acid-induced
        systemic lupus erythematosus. Oregon Health Sciences Uni-
        versity, Portland, OR. Published in *Rheumatic Diseases Clinics
        of North America*, Philadelphia, PA, May 1991, vol 17 p. 323-
        32. ISSN 0889-857X.

[15]   Effects of L-Canavanine on T cells may explain the induction
        of systemic lupus erythematosus by alfalfa. Alcocer-Varela, J.;
        Iglesias, A.; Llorente, L.; Alarcon-Segovia, D.; *Arthritis & Rheu-
        matism*, Hagerstown, MD, Jan, 1985, p.52-7. ISSN 0004-3591.

[16]   I. Emerit, A.M. Michelson, A. Levy, J.P. Camus, J. Emerit.
        Human Genetics, v 55, pg 341, 1980.

[17]   C.S. Foote, A. Autor, Ed. Pathology of Oxygen, *Academic
        Press*, pg 21-44. New York, 1982.

[18]   G. Rettura, C. Dattagupta, P. Listowsky, S.M. Levenson, E.
        Seifter, Federal Proc. Fed. American Society of Experimental
        Biology, v. 42, pg 786 1983.; M.M. Mathews-Roth, *Oncology*
        v39, pg 33, 1982.

[19]   A.C. Griffin, M.S. Arnott, J. Vaneys, Y.M. Wang, *Molecular Interrelations of Nutrition and Cancer*, pg 401-408. Raven, New York. 1982.

[20]   A.M. Novi, *Science* v 212, pg 541, 1981.

[21]   "The Health Effects of Nitrate, Nitrite and N-Nitroso Compounds." Committee on Nitrite and Alternative Curing Agents in Food. *National Academy of Sciences, National Academy Press,* Washington, DC 1981.

[22]   T Sugimura, M. Nagao. Mutagenicity: New Horizons in Genetic Toxicology. *Academic Press*, pg 72-88. New York, 1982.

[23]   "Protease Inhibitors May Block Tumor Spread", *The Cancer Reporter*, 1987, v.2,p.1-4.
       Troll, Et Al: "Protease Inhibitors: Possible Anticarcinogens in Edible Seeds". *Prostate*, 1983. v.4,p.345-349.

[24]   Marshall, Szczesniewski, and Johnston: "Dietary Alpha-Linolenic Acid and Prostaglandin Synthesis: A time Course Study." *American Journal of Clinical Nutrition,* 1983. v.38,p.895-900.

[25]   Mahan, Meunier, Newby, Young: "Prostaglandin E2 Production by EL4 Leukemia Cells from C57BL/6 Mice: Mechanism for Tumor Dissemination." *Journal of the National Cancer Institute*, 1985. v.74,p.191-195.

[26]   Setchell, Et Al: "Non-steroidal Estrogens of Dietary Origin: Possible Roles in Hormone Dependent Disease." *American Journal of Clinical Nutrition*, 1984. v.40,p.569-578.

[27]   Chihara, Et Al. "Fractionation and Purification of the Polysaccharides with Marked Anti-Tumor Activity Especially Lentinan From Lentinus Endoles Sing (An Edible Mushroom)." *Cancer Research*, 1970. v30. pg 2776-2781.

[28]   J. Hoey, C. Montvernay, R. Lambert, *American Journal of Epidemiology*, v113, pg 668. 1981.

[29]   Ulrich Abel, PhD, "Cytostatic Therapy of Advanced Epithelial Tumors: A Critique." An examination of the statistical relevance of chemotherapy in the treatment of cancer. *Der Spiegel*, vol 33, p. 174-176. 1991.

[30]   U.S. Department of Agriculture. Human Nutrition Information Service. *"Composition of Foods." Handbook #8*. 1963. by B.K. Watt and A.L. Merrill. *Handbook #8-20 Cereal Grains*, rev. 1989, D.L. Drake, S.E. Gebhardt, R.H. Matthews. *Handbook #8-16 Legumes*, rev. 1986, D.B. Haytowitz, R.H. Matthews. Handbook #8-12 Nuts & Seeds, rev. 1984. *Handbook #8-11 Vegetables*, rev. 1984, D.B. Haytowitz, R.H. Matthews. Supplements to Handbook #8, 1989,1990,1991.
        (2) E.W. Murphy, B.L. Watt and R.L. Rizek. U.S. Department of Agriculture Nutrient Data Bank. Associate Office of Analytic Chemistry. Journal. v57, pg 1198-1204.
        (3) Dr. Rolland McCready, USDA Western Regional Research Laboratory. Nutrients in Seeds and Sprouts of Alfalfa, Lentils, Mungs Beans and Soybeans. *Food Science*, 40:1008,1975

[30A]   Comparison charts created by the author from extracted data in [30].

[31]   E.C. Pfeiffer. "Protein changes during germination and earliest leaf growth." *Bio-Cynamics*, v47, pg 2. 1958.

[32]   D.S. Nandi, "Studies on the changes of free amino acids and B-Vitamin content of some leguminous seeds during germination." *Science and Culture*. v 23, pg 659. 1958.

[33]   N.K. Matheson and S. Strother. "Utilization of phytate by germinating wheat." *Biochemistry Journal,* v8, pg 1349. 1969.

[34]   Physician's Desk Reference. 47ed. 1993. Medical Economics
        Data, Montvale, NJ 07645. p. 883-885, 1816, 1397.

[35]   Eugene S. Wagner, Ph.D., Roger Noble, Ph.D. *"The Effect of
        Anti-oxidant Nutritional Support in Irradiated Mice."* Mun-
        cie Center for Medical Education, Ball State University, Mun-
        cie, Indiana. Indiana University School of Medicine.

[36]   Bell, E.A. Canavanine in the leguminosae. *Biochemistry Jour-
        nal* v. 75 p. 618-620, 1960.

[37]   Malinow, M.R., McLaughlin, P., Bardana, E.J., Craig, S.; Elimina-
        tion of toxicity from diets containing alfalfa seeds. *Food &
        Chemical Toxicology.* 1984. July 22. p. 583-587.

[38]   Peryt, B., Szymczyk, T, Lesca, P.; Mechanism of anti-
        mutagenicity of wheat sprout extracts. *Mutation Research*
        October 1992. #269, p. 201-215. Also: Peryt, B., Mioszewska,
        J., Tudek, B.; Anti-mutagenic effects of several subfractions of
        extract from wheat sprout toward benzo(a)pyrene induced
        mutagenicity in strain TA98 of salmonella typhimurium. *Muta-
        tion Research* 1988. v.206(2), p. 221-225.

[39]   Rosenthal, G.A.; The Biological effects and mode of action of
        L-canavanine, a structural analogue of L-arginine. *Quarterly
        Review of Biology,* 1977; v. 52, p. 155-178.

[40]   Malinow, M.R., Experimental models of atherosclerosis regres-
        sion. *Atherosclerosis.* 1983, August. v.48(2), p.105-108.

[41]   Malinow, M.R., Connor, W.E., McLaughlin, P. et al. Cholesterol
        and bile acid balance in Macaca fascicularis. Effects of alfalfa
        saponins. *Journal of Clinical Investigation,* New York, NY.
        1981. Jan. v.67(1), p. 156-162.

[42]   Malinow, M.R., McNulty, W.P., et al. Lack of toxicity of alfalfa
        saponins in cynomolgus macaques. *Journal of Medical Pri-
        matology.* 1982. v.11(2), p. 106-118.

[43]   Lancet, December 29, 1962.

[44]   Journal of Agricultural Food Chemistry. 1980. v.28, p.667-671.

[45]   Hutchens, Alma R., Indian Herbalogy of North America. Shambala Press, Boston. 1991.

[46]   Carper, Jean, The Food Pharmacy. Bantam Books, 1988. p.56-63, 132-138, 150-155, 198-206, 220-221, 246-250, 273-277.

[47]   Hoffmann, David, The Holistic Herbal. Element Books, Ltd. 1988.

[48]   Sanyal, S.N. "Ten Years of Research on an Oral Contraceptive from Pisum Sativum." *Science and Culture*, June, 1960. v.25-12, p.661-665.
         Beiler, J.M., et al. "Anti-Fertility Activity of Pisum Sativum." *Experimental Medicine and Surgery.* 1953. v.11, p.179-185.

[49]   Anderson, J.W., et al. "Dietary Fiber: Hyperlipidemia, Hypertension and Coronary Heart Disease." *American Journal of Clinical Nutrition.* 1986. v.81-10, p.907-919.
         Anderson, J.W., et al. "Hypocholesterolemic Effects of Oat-Bran and Bean Intake for Hypercholesterolemic Men." *American Journal of Clinical Nutrition.* 1984. v.40, p.1146-1155.

[50]   Messadi, D.V., et al. "Inhibition of Oral Carcinogenesis by a Protease Inhibitor." *Journal of the National Cancer Institute,* March 1986. v.76-3, p.447-452.

[51]   Troll, W., et al. "Soybean Diet Lowers Breast Tuomor Incidence in Irradiated Rats." *Carcinogenesis,* June 1980. v.1, p.469-472.

[52]   Bodia, A.K., et al. "Effect of the Essential Oil (active principle) of Garlic on serum Cholesterol, Plasma fibrinogen Whole Blood Coagulation Time and Fibrinolytic Activity in Alimen-

tary Lipaemia." *Journal of Associate Physicians Ind.*, 1974.
v22, p.267.
Bordia, A.K., et al. "Effect of Garlic on Blood Lipids in
Patients with Coronary Heart Disease." *Atherosclerosis*, 1977.
v.28,p.155.

[53]   Tsai, Y., et al. "Antiviral Properties of Garlic: In Vitro Effects
       on Influenza B, Herpes Simplex and Coxsackie Viruses."
       Planta Medca, October, 1985. v.4,p.460-461.

[54]   Bairacli Levy, Juliette de. *The Complete Herbal Handbook
       for Farm and Stable.* Published by Farber and Farber, Lon-
       don, England, 1952.

[55]   Mességué, Maurice. *Health Secrets of Plants and Herbs*, Wil-
       liam Morrow and Co. New York, NY, 1979.

[56]   Weissberger, L.E., Armstrong, M.K. Canavanine Analysis of
       Alfalfa Extracts by High Performance Liquid Chromatography
       Using Pre-Column Derivatization. *Journal of Chromato-
       graphic Science*, v.22, October, 1984.

[57]   Interview with Emil J. Bardana, by Steve Meyerowitz. 3/26/93

Are Sprouts Safe to Eat?

Salmonella Rate in Sprouts Make it Our Safest Food

In its January 10 1999 issue, the *Journal of the American Medical Association* (JAMA) described two incidences of salmonella contamination of alfalfa sprouts that took place in 1995. The objective of this study was to identify the source of the salmonella outbreaks. Because JAMA is a credible source of information, word soon spread through the national media that consumers should avoid eating alfalfa sprouts. Are they right? Are sprouts unsafe?

While scientific investigation takes some time, JAMA published this study 4 years after the incident giving the impression that this was the current state of affairs and unnecessarily scaring people away from this famous health food.

Since the 1995 outbreaks, all sprouting seeds have been subject to a strict screening and purification process and major importers and distributors now offer a microbiological test certificate for their seeds. Salmonella and e-coli contamination is extremely rare. Nevertheless, growers now use an EPA approved pasteurization process, similar to that of the nation's water supply, to achieve a 99.8% reduction of salmonella and E. Coli. Put another way, if an extremely rare occurrence of tainted seed should occur, there would be only a 0.02% probability that such bacteria could survive. There is no chlorine residue in the sprouts (unlike our drinking water). But the environmentally conscious sprout industry is researching non-chlorine pasteurization methods with the FDA at the National Center for Food Safety and Technology in Illinois. Many sprout growers display a new "Food Safety Seal of Approval," indicating that their products were certified by independent third party safety auditors. The sprout industry works closely with the FDA and USDA.

Some distortion of the facts may have turned sprouts into an undeserved scapegoat for food contamination. JAMA confesses to "only 133 reported cases," but they claim a probable "20,000 affected." This only fuels public fears. Let's put the risk of getting salmonella from sprouts in prospective. Every year, according to the CDC, 4 million people contract salmonella from poultry, meat, eggs, milk and fresh fruits and vegetables. US sprout growers ship 1.4 billion 4-ounce servings of sprouts every year, but over the last 40 years there have been fewer than 2,000 cases of contamination linked to sprouts (Calif. Dept. of Health). Yes, JAMA correctly points out that sprouts have a greater potential to harbor microbes because they are uncooked. But this is the same risk posed by fresh produce. In a recent five year period, there were 41 outbreaks due to fresh produce, one of them, a 1989 shipment of cantaloupes from Mexico, caused 25,000 salmonellosis cases (CDC). Yet, in over 40 years, sprouts have had a total of 12 outbreaks—4 of them traced to the same 1995 tainted seed. In the same 5 year period, 195 outbreaks were caused by meat and poultry and 178 by seafood. Every year, the CDC documents fatalities caused by foods such as peanuts, milk, eggs and shellfish, but there has never been any from sprouts.

In a given year, getting hit by lightning (1.29 people per million) is more likely than contracting E. coli (1.1 people per million) from meat, poultry, shellfish, milk, eggs and produce combined. Since produce represents the smallest risk of these foods (41 outbreaks in 5 years) and since sprouts represent an even smaller risk than produce (12 outbreaks in 40 years), sprouts are statistically our safest food. Since the National Cancer Institute and the National Institutes of Health want us to eat 5 fresh foods per day, and since the phytochemicals in sprouts are a proven cancer protector (Johns Hopkins University 1997), the benefits of eating sprouts far outweigh the contamination risks.

The U.S. food and water supply will never be completely free of harmful bacteria. Nothing grown in nature is sterile. But most of the microorganisms found naturally on fresh foods are harmless. Overall, Americans can have confidence that their food supply is safe. To this end, sprout growers are working diligently with the FDA and USDA to ensure that sprouts are not only one of the healthiest foods you can eat, but also one of the safest.

Note: *If you feel the need to sterilize your home grown sprouts, use hydrogen peroxide and follow the instructions on page 55 and 56. For chlorine pasteurization, soak your seeds for 10 minutes in 1/4 cup water with 1 Tbsp of Clorox bleach.*

Latest News about Sprouts

Antioxidants Help Turn Back the Aging-Clock

U.S. Department of Agriculture researchers at Tufts University have slowed—and reversed—the aging process in rats by feeding them diets fortified with certain fruits and vegetables. "We prevented both some brain and some behavioral changes that one normally sees in these rats when they hit 15 months."—Jim Joseph, USDA.

Some of the foods with the highest orac value—the measure of antioxidants in foods—were garlic, kale, spinach, brussel sprouts and alfalfa sprouts. According to the study, middle-aged rats fed a high-orac diet had better memory. Even more amazing, the older rats began walking like younger rats. Researchers credit the free radical-fighting antioxidants found in sprouts and the other high orac foods. "It's pretty well accepted that aging is due to the production of free radicals, so anything we can do nutritionally to provide additional antioxidants is likely to protect us in the process of aging," —USDA researcher Ron Prior.

Antioxidant Capacity of Tea and Common Vegetables, by Cav, GH, Sofic, E, Prior, RL. Journal of Agricultural and Food Chemistry, 44: (11) 3426-3431 Nov. 1996.

Alfalfa Sprouts and the Prevention of Menopausal Symptoms, Osteoporosis, Cancer and Heart Disease

Studies in humans, animals and cell cultures suggest that dietary phytoestrogens play an important role in prevention of menopausal symptoms, osteoporosis, cancer and heart disease. Phytoestrogens are plant estrogens and include isoflavones, coumestans, and lignans. Alfalfa clover and soybean sprouts, along with oilseeds such as flaxseed are the best dietary sources. While not true estrogens, they are similar enough to induce a host of significant effects. One of these is an adaptogenic or balancing effect. In other words, alfalfa is ideally suited for conditions resulting from either too little or too much estrogen. These phytoestrogens have been used as elements in the holistic treatment of low estrogen conditions such as hot flashes, menopause and preventive osteoporosis, as well as excess estrogen conditions such as premenstrual syndrome

(PMS), fibrocystic breasts, and estrogen–responsive cancers of the breast and uterus. These relatively weak-acting phytoestrogens compete for binding sites with the stronger true estrogens reducing the conditions of estrogen excess or providing an adequate supply where needed.

Alfalfa contains other therapeutic phytochemicals such as an analog related to TRH, the Thyrotropin Releasing Hormone. This TRH compound works via the hypothalmus to inhibit prolactin and thus has the potential to treat both hypothyroidism and cystic ovaries.

Another biologically active compound in alfalfa, flavone, has the ability to relax smooth muscle tissue. Because it is also not easily absorbed in the digestive tract, it is ideal for cramps or colic.

High Cholesterol

Alfalfa sprouts as well as alfalfa extracts and powder have demonstrated the ability to both reduce cholesterol and the plaque build-up inside artery walls that cause atherosclerosis. Alfalfa appears to lower triglycerides and low density lipoproteins (LDL's) while not significantly lowering the good high density (HDL's). This appears to be a function of the phytosterols and saponins in alfalfa. Phytosterols are plant sterols (steroids) that compete with cholesterol and decrease it. Chickens, rats and monkeys fed the equivalent of an average American intake of cholesterol, had their cholesterol reduced when alfalfa was added to their diet. In another study, the saponins from alfalfa also reduced the cholesterol and triglycerides of rats when alfalfa was added to their diets.

Maintaining alfalfa and other sprouts in the diet, along with a general program of holistic health, exercise and fresh vegetables, can treat and prevent many conditions that would otherwise require more expensive invasive therapies. Botanical medicines were the original medicines of the Greeks, the Chinese, Native Americans and many other cultures until the recent advent of 20th century drugs. Speaking 400 years before the birth of Christ, Hippocrates, the "father of medicine" said it best: "Let your food be your medicine and your medicine be your food."

Dietary Phytoestrogens, by Xu Kurtzer, MS. The Annual Review of Nutrition, 17:353-381 1997.
Clinical Application Medicago sativa extracts, by Paul Reilly, N.D. Journal of Naturopathic Medicine. Volume 1, No. 1, 1999.

INDEX

Who Is This Sproutman?

Steve Meyerowitz began his journey to better health in 1975 to correct a lifelong chronic condition of severe allergies and asthma. After two months of eating a living foods, vegetarian diet, his symptoms disappeared. After almost 20 years of disappointment with conventional medicine, Steve restored his health through his own program of purification, lifestyle adjustment, exercise, fasting, juicing and living foods.

Over the years, he has lived on and experimented with many so called 'extreme' diet/lifestyles including, raw foods, fruitarianism, sprouts, dairy and flourless vegetarianism and fasting. In 1977, he was pronounced "Sproutman" by *Vegetarian Times Magazine* in a feature article that explored his innovative sprouting ideas and recipes.

After 10 years as a music and comedy entertainer, he made a complete lifestyle change for his health. In 1980, he opened *The Sprout House*, a "no-cooking school" in New York City. There, he began a formal program of teaching kitchen gardening and the preparation of gourmet sprouted and vegetarian foods. Steve has invented two home sprouters, the *Flax Sprout Bag* and *the Kitchen Garden Salad Grower* and was the founder of the Sprout House, a company supplying home growing kits and a full line of organic sprouting seeds.

Steve has been featured on the *Home Shopping Network, TV Food Network, in Prevention, Organic Gardening and Flower & Garden Magazines.* In 3 minutes on QVC, 953 people ordered his Cookbook and Salad Grower.

Steve and his family, including three little sprouts, now live and breathe the fresher air of the Berkshire mountains.

Other Books

By Steve Meyerowitz
www.Sproutman.com

Water the Ultimate Cure
Discover Why Water is the Most Important Ingredient in your Diet and Find Out Which Water is Right for You. 2001.

Power Juices Super Drinks
Quick, Delicious Recipes to Reverse and Prevent Disease. 2000.

Wheatgrass Nature's Finest Medicine
The Complete Guide to Using Grass Foods & Juices to Revitalize Your Health. 1999.

Food Combining and Digestion
101 Ways to Improve Digestion 2002.

Sproutman's Kitchen Garden Cookbook
Sprout Breads, Cookies, Soups, Salads & 250 other Low Fat, Dairy Free Vegetarian Recipes. 1999.

Juice Fasting & Detoxification
Use the Healing Power of Fresh Juice to Feel Young and Look Great. 2002.

Sproutman's "Turn the Dial" Sprout Chart
A Field Guide to Growing and Eating Sprouts. 1998.

Clinician's Complete Reference to Complementary/Alternative Medicine.
Steve Meyerowitz, co-author. Edited by Donald W. Novey, M.D. 2000.

Sprouts the Miracle Food
The Complete Guide to Sprouting. 1999.